By The Seat of Our Pants

Also Written by Mary Anne Tegge Brunton

One Dog One Trick

By The Seat of Our Pants

Mary Anne Tegge Brunton

iUniverse, Inc.
Bloomington

By The Seat of Our Pants

iUniverse books may be ordered through booksellers or by contacting:

iUniverse
1663 Liberty Drive
Bloomington, IN 47403
www.iuniverse.com
1-800-Authors (1-800-288-4677)

ISBN: 978-1-4759-8263-3 (sc)
ISBN: 978-1-4759-8264-0 (ebk)

Library of Congress Control Number: 2013905104

Printed in the United States of America

iUniverse rev. date: 03/25/2013

Contents

PART I

Gone Fishing

PART II

Europe

Germany

France

Spain

Italy

England

This book is dedicated with all my heart, my love, and my joy to Jim (Dad), my husband who *snatched* me from the secure arms of the Galveston Art Center and propelled me into the spectacular world of California, Canada, and Europe. For over twenty years, we have loved and laughed our way through nonstop adventures.

I am forever grateful Jim had the patience not to scream when I had map-reading failures while entering Switzerland, by mistake, twice within an hour. Also, I am forever thankful we never had to spend a night in the back of the car due to lack of hotel reservations—but close. *By the seat of our pants* we flew, and I'd do it all over again in a heartbeat.

Acknowledgments

There are times when writing a book the words flow like water rushing down a high-country river. When these times occur, I think little of sentence structure, punctuation, and spelling. As they say, I just go with the flow. It was then I knew I needed an editor with a gentle touch and a sense of humor. These are traits I found in my friend Bill Bishop. Bill became interested in my endeavor and thus generously and graciously gave me his time, knowledge, and suggestions along the way. I am forever grateful for his constant interest and wise guidance.

Introduction

With promises of streets of gold where the weather is good, Dad (Jim) sweeps Mom (Mary Anne) off her Texan feet and sets her down in sunny Southern California. Conquering Los Angeles freeways, meeting new friends, and adjusting to a casual lifestyle were the beginning of a life of adventures. As Dad habitually has wanderlust in his eyes, he introduces Mom to the wonderful worlds of fishing and European travel.

Fishing the streams of Wyoming to the Pacific Rim of Canada and on to the lakes of Alaska proved to be challenging efforts along with escaping the wrath of Dad's fishing guide, Adonis Doug. Learning to understand the operation of an RV, with instructions given by a close relative of an army drill sergeant, proved to be somewhat intimidating, especially the issues that concerned the draining of water tanks. Also, we learned that Colorado sheriffs are not sympathetic toward speeding automobiles, as jail seems to be the only option for that violation.

Europe presents its own set of challenging adventures. Driving the autobahn and being lost; reading maps written in foreign languages and being lost; appearing in Switzerland, twice within an hour while attempting to be in Germany, obviously lost again. Menu struggles, currency struggles, foreign language GPS struggles are only a few of the trials we experienced while driving the roads of Europe with no *efficient map reader* on board. Also, learning that Hotel Dieu and Hotel de Ville were not hotels at all shattered dreams of our knowing the French language.

In contrast to the pieces devoted to the challenges of auto travel and NO HOTEL RESERVATIONS in foreign countries, I have included warm and fuzzy moments where the beauty and love of special times will warm your heart. If the Palio horse race on the streets of Sienna doesn't run us down, perhaps we will, again, spend another perfect Christmas in Rothenburg ob der Tauber.

In this period of hard economic times, I find it a bit difficult to share these glimpses of frivolous expenditure. But as one of my favorite authors Peter Mayle would say, what would life be without the occasional treat?

Prologue

Streets of Gold

Welcome to Galveston. A sleepy little town/city located on the Gulf of Mexico. I loved walking along the waterfront after a day of working at the art center; however, summers can be brutal with high humidity and temperatures soaring into the nineties and occasionally above.

Dad and I were married on July 3, 1992, at the county courthouse in Galveston. Previous communication told us to bring thirty-five dollars cash, as checks were not accepted. After paying thirty-five dollars for the license, plus a nice tip to the judge, who turned out to be a former college roommate of my cousin, the deed was done. This was followed by a marriage license issued that looked like we had won it at a circus carnival—bows, bells, and doves imprinted.

Since Dad was a California resident and surely not used to heat and humidity, he was more than anxious to take me West "where the streets are paved with gold." I had a bit of worry as Dad struggled up and down three flights of stairs while lugging my belongings. After a quick tepid shower, he assured me he would live another day. That was good news, as I would have found it difficult to explain to his two children that after one day of marital bliss, I had done their dad in. After packing my new Ford station wagon, complete with two dogs, Maggie and Buckets, we were off on our first adventure. I must say that happiness for Dad was Galveston in our rearview mirror.

Oh, yes, I believe it is time to say I have no idea when we began calling each other Dad and Mom. After several years of marriage, it occurred to me that we had adopted those names without ever realizing it.

After three days and three nights on the road, we arrived at Dad's house in California, where we were greeted by a young Mexican girl who lived on site and spoke no English. She was absolutely terrified of me and believed I was going to send her on her way back to Mexico. Amparo soon learned I needed all the help I could get, and we became fast friends. She lived with us until she married and her daughter became school-age. She now has three children and her husband owns a successful business. We continue to stay in touch to this day.

California brought its own set of adventures to me. There were new markets, different flowers for gardens, beastly freeways, and casual dress to the extreme, only to name a few.

My first encounter with extreme casual dress was Christmas Eve. Dad and I were dressed to the nines, complete with fur coat, and on our way to a lovely restaurant prior to our going to church. After being seated, I noticed a woman wearing jeans and a Mickey Mouse sweatshirt. (Somehow I could hear my good friend Nina whispering something in my ear about fruits and nuts). All I can say is that most women in Texas have a little black dress and pearls, and her escort owns a proper tie and jacket. This was probably my first culture shock, right along with domestic help calling me by my first name.

Negotiating the freeways was a fearsome and life-threatening project. I quickly learned that drivers sometimes shoot other drivers when suffering spells of road rage. Also, if one driver happens to be driving the speed limit at 70 mph, they are banished to the slow lane with lots of finger waving—85 mph and higher is the norm. I stayed lost a good bit of the time, as there were no GPS systems then, or at least I hadn't learned about them. A really good day of driving for me was making a minimum of wrong turns and not too many honking horns all while gripping the steering wheel with white-knuckle force. And true happiness for me was a freeway sign that read "La Canada/Flintridge next three exits." That meant I had home in my sights. One personal goal I have is never to drive to the Los Angeles airport. So far, I have achieved that goal.

The weather was another issue with which to deal. For the most part, the weather in California is mild and sunny. We actually have a rainy season, unlike Houston and Galveston, where there is more annual rainfall than Seattle and can rain any month of the year—and usually does. However, along with the Southern California weather comes snow in the local mountains, mudslides following a heavy rainfall, and Santa Ana winds that bring a high chance of wildfires.

My first experience with a wildfire arrived in the middle of the night with helicopters flying overhead and nonstop TV news alerts. We could see the flames in the not-too-far distance. With the knowledge of possible evacuation, I began to make a few plans. As Dad was away at his office, I decided to make myself at the ready. First, I gathered provisions for Maggie and Buckets, along with proper pet carriers. In order to make certain I could escape with my "fine jewelry," I put on all of it at one time. I often wondered what a fireman might have thought had he come to the door to find such a sight as myself. Nevertheless, I was ready to go if necessary. Fortunately, we remained out of the extreme danger area.

Many years later I actually did have to do a fire evacuation. This time I escaped with the computer that held banking and financial records, one dog, two cats, and the aforementioned jewelry. On this evacuation, I learned two amazing things. The first being that in a road evacuation, it can take approximately five and a half hours to drive a hundred miles in the dark on unfamiliar highways. The second amazement was that I learned it is possible for a cat to meow nonstop, without taking a breath, for five and a half hours. This adventure is one I should not like to repeat, but remember, "the weather is good."

Another wonderful piece of excitement is the earthquake, which seems to visit with monotonous regularity. This lovely bit of thrill happened for the first time about six months after I moved to la-la land. Dear Lord—in the middle of the night I thought the house would shake down. Scared, you bet I was! We survived with only a broken window or two, many crooked pictures, dogs that slept through it all, and cats who lived under the bed for days at a time. Since then, I have had the dubious pleasure of "earthquake life" many times over. All I say to this is give me a good ole hurricane anytime; just leave those earthquakes alone. However, I must remember "the weather is good."

All in all, life in California is great. Young grandchildren love to come for a visit. We have Disneyland, wild animal parks, Tijuana shopping, and even a Jay Leno show for a birthday surprise treat, plus a round or two of golf at Torrey Pines for my golfing grandson.

There is a constant supply of theatrical productions, movie openings, sporting events, and Hollywood gossip to keep one entertained. Plants and flowers grow easily here and almost year-round. One can sit on their patio, wearing shorts and flip-flops, and see snow on the mountaintops just beyond. And here, outdoor grilling has become an art form. In fact, outdoor life is almost always available, for there is little rain. Dad keeps reminding me that this is the desert with just a little water splashed on it. Spanish is the second language, and if one does not even have a slight command of it, one will find themselves conversationally challenged. Good grapes are grown here and fine wine is produced. Some European wine snobs are thrilled when California wine is imported to their country, I have been told.

Dad loves California and we will always live here. The taxes are high and house prices are outrageous, but he likes that California is on the cutting edge of many venues. Actually, I have not noticed all the streets being "paved with gold," but I do know that "the weather is good."

PART I

Gone Fishing

The Armchair Fisherman

I, as well as perhaps you, have heard many times that every hour one spends fishing adds another year to one's life or something like that. Anyway, if that were halfway true, my father would have lived to be 275 years old; and Dad, who is still alive, will probably live to be 300, or maybe more.

However, the best fishing story I know is about my friend Tom, who is the ultimate *armchair fisherman*. Tom and his wonderful wife, Ida Jo, my best friend, have a lovely condominium on the Gulf of Mexico in Texas. Dad and I have visited them there and have grown to understand how much they love it. I believe Tom is happiest being near or on the water, whereas Ida Jo truly loves their Texas ranch, complete with cattle and bluebonnets. They seem to enjoy the best of both worlds.

Tom has all the best proper fishing equipment—rods, reels, artificial baits, and, of course, a sleek and sturdy boat. He keeps his rods and reels squeaky clean and highly polished. His boat is a craft of beauty. And his most treasured fishing possession is his LOUNGE CHAIR, located in his lovely living room overlooking the water.

To my knowledge, Tom has never personally used any of the above-mentioned equipment for fishing; however, fishing is his very special hobby, and he has chosen to enjoy it from the comfort of his luxurious reclining chair while sipping a glass of good wine while others go about the business of launching boats, buying bait, and cleaning fish.

I don't know if Tom will get extra life-year credit for his type of fishing, but I think the wine should help.

Living Large in a Rented RV

Wyoming

There are four important *F*s in Dad's life—fishing, food, flying radio-controlled airplanes, and football. Depending on the season of the year or the time of the day, one *F* may take precedent over another. The food *F* needs regular attention at least three times a day. The football *F* consumes our Saturdays and Sundays during the fall and early winter. The flying *F* is a rather new addition for Dad, who would like to fly his airplane twice a day every day, if weather and time permitted. The fishing *F* is a whole other thing. I do believe this is Dad's greatest love.

So let's take fishing. When the spring rain showers decrease and the flowers start to bloom, Dad's eyes begin to glaze over with dreams of fishing, and most any kind of fishing will work—mountain stream fishing, salmon fishing in Canada, and lake fishing in Alaska, to name a few. Actually, any old pond, lake, or river will work as long as there is water and an occasional fish. Dad's even tried a bit of redfish and trout fishing in the Gulf of Mexico, off the Texas coast. There the fishing was fun, but truly I believe he liked eating the Texas Gulf shrimp most of all. Why, he's even routed airline travel through Houston just so he could down a few shrimp between flights. Oh well, that's another story and a different *F* factor.

Mountain stream fishing was a new experience for me. However, Dad has done this his entire life in the rivers of Colorado. His method of stream fishing was something I had never seen before.

He would toss out the line and slowly pull it in by hand, as opposed to an actual reel cast. He called this Indian fishing and was learned from his father. I called it strange and inefficient. Why in the world were fishing reels invented if you chose to pull all the line by hand? However, in time, I did master the style and learned to work the trout pools as well. And guess what? I even had success using a fishing reel—imagine that!

While the shine was still on the honeymoon, I was introduced to stream fishing, with the ultimate goal of the Tongue River in the Big Horn Mountains of Wyoming. These mountains have a different beauty of their own. Their claim to fame is poor old General Custer, who met his maker at the Battle of the Little Bighorn. After viewing the battlegrounds, I agree with historians that General Custer made some very bad decisions. Also, I'm not too sure the Indians really got much, as the fought-over land is somewhat barren.

In those days, descending on the Big Horn Mountain Range was no easy trick, as we first flew to Denver and then drove to Burgess Junction, with a stop between to have hamburgers at the Busy Bee restaurant in Buffalo, Wyoming. The Busy Bee was owned and run by two round and mature sisters. Their method of cooking and serving was to cook one hamburger at a time. It was almost impossible to have a meal together as one burger would be stone-cold while waiting for the other to cook. However, I must admit the burgers were special. We made this stop in Buffalo, as it was something that Dad had always done in many previous years. As you can see, Dad is a traditionalist at heart.

After finishing our burgers and enjoying every bite, off we go to Burgess Junction, Wyoming, and the Bear Lodge. This indeed was a sight to behold. Being situated in the middle of the beautiful Big Horn Mountains no way compensated for the rather decrepit Bear Lodge.

The dining room was fairly acceptable, and, depending if the fry cook were knowledgeable or just there to spend time drying out, a decent meal could be had from time to time. The saving grace was Big Mike, who could produce the most delicious pies if the mood struck him to do so, which was somewhat sporadic. The Bear Lodge had one telephone, which was a six-party line located in the dining area (and I use the term "dining area" loosely). I'm not sure they knew television was even a medium, as there was none. Dad said "not to fear, the rooms are clean." I must say, everyone has their own definition of a clean room. I'll just have to leave it at that.

However, nothing in my life had ever prepared me for the assault on the lodge by a motorcycle gang—possibly Hell's Angels. Why, I was even invited to take a ride on a Harley driven by Mad Dog. Invitation refused! Never have I seen so many bikers gather together while using a continuous stream of foul language. There were male bikers, female bikers, fat bikers, very fat bikers, and morbidly obese bikers. Their obvious goal was to make sure there was no alcoholic beverage of any kind remaining in the county when they left the next day.

I'm certain they achieved their goal, as one drunken male attempted to crawl in our bedroom window sometime in the night. This may have been the one who was morbidly obese, as he got somewhat stuck trying to get in. One female in the next room broke her leg while performing a sexual act of some unimaginable skill, and the remaining riders barfed their way through to dawn. Obviously, a good time was had by all. For me, I had fantasies of looking for prescription drugs to ease my acute anxiety.

With the break of day, Dad took pity on me and said we would leave this den of iniquity for more suitable surroundings. We did leave, and it probably saved our young marriage. I must add that little girls who have been carefully raised in the South are not prepared or equipped for such adventures

Escaping the jaws of the Bear Lodge, we began making our way to Boulder, Colorado, so I could meet Dad's sister, Betty. As in many of our travels, we hit a rather big bump in the road, namely a Colorado sheriff. Dad likes to drive at a speed that makes me close my eyes from time to time, and this Mach 1 pace caught the eye of a rookie sheriff, who was quite eager to hand out tickets. The sheriff pulled us over and inspected Dad's driver's license, whereby he said, and I quote, "***BAD NEWS, YOU ARE GOING TO JAIL.***" With that, I exclaimed in major hysteria mode, "***WE ARE WHAT?***" It turns out that there is no reciprocity between Colorado and California. That is bad news, to be sure.

It is now time that I share with you the fact that I find it necessary, at times, to speak in all CAPS, sometimes even in ***BOLD*** letters. Also, I have learned that *italics* is preferred to show emphasis. As I continue, I shall work on that, but I will miss my quote and dash marks.

Now back to Colorado. After a bit of lawyer-card flashing and Colorado Superior Court credentials, we were allowed to mail the proper fine due while being escorted by the sheriff, who then officially observed our dropping the envelope into a mailbox.

Finally on the road again, we were once more off to Boulder. This side trip was especially for me to meet my new sister-in-law, Betty. I have never had a sister-in-law before, so this was very exciting and a little frightening, I might add

I'm sure that Betty was more than slightly curious about me. She was a retired English teacher, and she cleverly gave me English tests during our conversations. These little tests continued throughout her life. The last test, cunningly constructed, was for me to find the grammatical error in the University of Colorado newsmagazine. Betty could hardly imagine a well-known university distributing a publication containing grammatical errors. Thank you, Lord, I found it and she never tested me again.

Gratefully, I always seemed to pass. I must say Betty never said she was testing me; she was way too smug for that. Actually, I believe she wanted to be certain I was smart enough for her "baby brother" a.k.a. Dad. In fact, she used to phone us and say, "I just wanted to have an intelligent conversation, and by the way, how are you?"

Betts, as we called her, was a Colorado University football fan. Her method of watching the home games was to wait until halftime and then walk to the stadium and sneak in to find an empty seat. I suppose everyone has a bit of larceny in their hearts.

Betts and I shared our love of books and sports. If I had lived closer to her, I'm sure we would have become great friends. Dad and I do miss her regular phone calls when she would share with us her magnificent description of Colorado snowfalls, leaf-changing colors, and springtime daffodils in bloom.

Betty was a rationalizer of the "first water." She was a "closet" smoker or, rather, a closed-bathroom-door smoker. Betty said that smoking helps her breathe, as she had a touch of self-diagnosed asthma. Also, on our annual drive in the mountains to see the quaking aspen trees in full golden color, she always had a grand supply of hard candy, lemon drops, etc., as she believed the candy kept her ears clear in the mountain altitude.

This brings to mind a story from a good friend of mine, Mary by name, told to me some years ago. Mary and husband Al had three family members, all senior in years, who lived together in a house. There was a mother, a mother-in-law, and an uncle. The mother-in-law was the "queen" and spent her days reading the latest tabloids. The mother appeared to do most of the work—cooking, cleaning, etc. Daily, Uncle Ed's job was to go out of doors to pick up pecans, when truthfully, he was going to the garage to drink his one beer—I think—for the day. "The girls," as they liked to be called, suspected this and finally told Uncle Ed he could bring his beer into the kitchen, put it in the fridge, and drink in the comfort of his favorite living room chair. Well, Uncle Ed had drunk his beer at a garage-warm temperature for so long he did not like the cold beer. So back it went to the garage for the rest of his days. Funny how seniors have their set ways. Whether it be smoking in the bathroom or drinking beer in the garage, they like to think they are fooling us all.

Since the Bear Lodge proved to be totally unacceptable to me for future stream-fishing trips, I set about finding an alternate choice of shelter, as I could see this fishing adventure was to become an annual event. After much searching, I discovered that an RV might be just right for us. We could fly to Billings Montana, rent the RV, and be by the mountain stream for early evening fishing all on the same day. You could have your bed, bathroom, kitchen, and sitting room all streamside. Life is good

Our first experience with a large RV was thrilling to say the least. The agency attendant spent an excessive amount of time explaining how to park the vehicle on flat ground—just watch the bubble on the dial to be sure it rests in the middle. This is to ensure that the fridge will work properly and continue to produce a cold temperature. May I remind you that we are in the Big Horn Mountains, and mountains are not flat, generally.

Lesson two—propane. This is important. One needs propane for cooking, heating, cooling, and who knows what else. Propane refills are not found on every mountain turn, so we agreed to be very frugal in our use.

Third, and probably the most important, is the care and emptying of the wastewater and gray water tanks. These tanks are workhorses for RVs. The tanks receive water from dish washing, showers, hand washing, and, most importantly, toilet waste. Above all, always save space for emergencies. Also, keep on the lookout for tank clean-out stations, as they are few and far between and occasionally are not to be found at all.

The RV agency was thorough in their instructions of how to maintain the above-mentioned features. In fact, we began our first RV adventure simply terrified we would use all the propane, kill the fridge, and overflow the water tanks. We were hesitant to use air-conditioning or heating for fear of running out of propane. Little did we know the tank held enough propane to cool or heat a family of four for about six months—while cooking nonstop. Also, when one is in the mountains, there is precious little flat ground on which to park your RV. There must be a little wiggle room there, however, as the fridge always seemed to work well.

As to the wastewater reservoirs, it is a good thing to keep your eye on them. There are two jobs involved when emptying the water tanks. One job is to turn the valves that are mounted on the side of the vehicle. I'm certain a preschool child could master this job in record time, which makes me wonder why Dad thought it needed a *lawyer/physicist* to deal with the task of turning the valve. I mean the valve is either *off* or *on*—how complicated is that? The other job is to physically hold the drain hose, full of waste, into a receptacle in the ground with the holder person bent over at a forty-five-degree angle for about twenty minutes. Would you like to guess whose job it was to hold the hose to the ground? You guessed it—MOI!

Dad and I have many wonderful memories of our Wyoming fishing trips—beautiful meadows ablaze with wildflowers, the gentle ripple of a mountain stream, and deer and moose grazing just outside the RV windows.

There are two vivid memories that are much more amusing today than when they occurred. Once in a stream of clear, cold water, I attempted to step on a rock, barely submerged, to get a bit closer to a trout pool. That "barely submerged" rock was actually about three-feet deep, and I ended up with wet blue jeans, thigh high. Stream water can be very cold and deceiving. Did I say *COLD*?

The second and most memorable of all occurred on a cloudy and cold afternoon. Prior to Dad's leaving to fish, I said, "If we were in Colorado high country, I would say it was going to snow." Well, it did! Did I say *SNOW*? Mind you, this was early September. Hurriedly, we moved our RV to the campground and watched the largest snowflakes I've ever seen float into a beautiful snowscape. At first the snow was fun, at least for me, but after four days of watching the snow pile up, and I mean pile up, with no fishing and lots of gin rummy, we began to wonder if we were there for the winter. Also, you really must like/love the person with whom you are confined or there could be temptations of murder by knife, as that is the only weapon on board, and it was there to clean fish.

Finally, the snow subsided and we *FISHTAILED* our RV all the way to the infamous Bear Lodge for a hot dinner and shower. We were given a newly remodeled room, the honeymoon suite we were told, complete with whirlpool tub and king-size bed. Not in the class of the Oriental Mandarin Hotel in Munich but certainly a five-star comfort after days of living in our house on wheels. Funny how our Wyoming fishing began and, years later, ended at the Bear Lodge. By the way, there were still no private telephones.

Adonis Doug and the Salmon Slayers

Bamfield, Canada

Salmon fishing in Canada has always been one of Dad's loves. He fished there for years before I entered his life. At some point, I must have told him I liked to fish, for once again I was included in a fishing festivity for which I was unfamiliar.

This adventure was accomplished by first flying from Los Angeles to Seattle. Upon arrival, we rented a car and drove to Vancouver for a brief stop to visit a lawyer associate. The associate then reminded us that this was Friday and the ferryboat line could be quite long. Well, let me tell you, that associate was right on target. Never had I seen such a line of automobiles except for maybe in the fire evacuation that I mentioned earlier. After thinking about it, the evacuation traffic did move at about 10 mph where the ferry line ***DID NOT MOVE AT ALL.***

After establishing ourselves in the proper ferry line, we began our wait, and wait it was. I gnawed on a package of raw carrots, completed a needlepoint Christmas ornament for my grandchild, and took a very long nap. When I awakened, I realized the line had not moved one inch! At that point other bored and restless people began to leave their cars and jog—some with their dogs. After a time, one jogger came by to say that he thought all hotel rooms in Nanaimo were sold out. Nanaimo was the ferry's destination. Being one to never give up, I left the car, found a pay phone, and called Best Western reservations—and behold, there was one room left. Let me tell you, no penthouse suite in Las Vegas could have looked so beautiful to me. I thought I had been saved and gone to heaven.

Next morning we were off to Bamfield, with a brief stop in Port Alberny for provisions. Coffee, junk food, bacon, bread, and wine seemed to be on the top of the grocery list. Bumping along on an old dirt-logging road for many miles, we bounced our way into Bamfield. It was then I was told our cabin was across an inlet, and a boat was necessary in order to get us there. Fine, but what boat? Dad said not to worry, one will be by before too long. And sure enough one came.

I must step aside and share a story that took place many years ago. Being from Texas, originally, I did my fair share of deer hunting. Texans hunt on deer leases that are generally working ranches. This particular lease was about 1,500 acres and fairly remote. A dear friend, Jerry, who always had the luck of the Irish, used a dilapidated old Jeep for deer-lease transportation. One day the Jeep broke down in the middle of *nowhere*, and wouldn't you know it, along came an auto tow truck to the rescue. Keep in mind, this lease was on fenced private property. I have no idea how and why the tow truck got there. There were no cell phones to call for help. But just like Dad said the boat would be by for us, Jerry's tow truck also magically appeared.

The Bamfield craft was piloted by a self-proclaimed fishing guide, Terry by name. The boat closely resembled the notorious *African Queen*, forever memorialized in the movie by the same name. Also, I might add that Terry and his wife, Sue, owned the cabin in which we were going to stay. At this point, I should also add that there was no way in the world I would go in Terry's boat for our fishing trip. I was more than a little nervous just crossing the inlet. Fortunately, we had Doug in our future.

After loading our supplies and crossing the inlet, we were ushered to our cabin. Well, this in and of itself was a vision to behold. The beds were bunk in style. Fortunately, there were enough beds that we didn't have to scale Mount Everest in order to climb to the top bunk. I was somewhat confused as to the choice of sofa design—pink satin fabric with roses embroidered randomly. A curious choice for a fishing cabin, I thought. (It might have been okay for an old English cottage). The heating unit was a challenge—too hot or too cold. We finally learned that if you got under the bed comforter and stuck your rear end out onto the cold wall, you could balance hot and cold. Logic beats physics every time.

Another and perhaps the most challenging was the bathroom shower curtain. No matter where you positioned yourself in the shower, the cold curtain *GRABBED* you at every body part. This gave new meaning to the words "quick shower" or "in and out quick like a rabbit."

Signs—let me tell you there were signs. There were more signs than a public swimming pool. Put the paper in this can, the food waste in that can, coffee grounds in another can, and products containing foil in the final can. I'm not sure I ever mastered the sign test, but I tried. I will say that Terry and wife Sue checked the cans daily and left notes if they found violations of improper use.

But now to the fun part of our trip. Fishing. At least I thought it was to be fun. First, you get up at four thirty in the morning—and it is still dark outside. After walking down a path you spy the boat complete with the fishing guide, Doug. Doug was rather an Adonis in appearance. He had blond wavy hair and was tall and lean but was orthodontically challenged. Never have I seen such a disappointed look, which Doug showed when he discovered Dad had a fishing companion, and a *FEMALE* at that. Doug soon learned that I was *THE WIFE* and his wonderful fishing days alone with Dad were history. I believe, in Doug's mind, that if he made the trip as uncomfortable for me as possible, I would stay in the cabin for the duration of the trip.

Once on board the craft, we took off at about Mach 1 speed in search of finding king salmon. We approached the infamous Point Beall spot where Doug assured us we would catch salmon, as that was the only fish he allowed on his boat. I shudder to think how many beautiful sea bass we tossed back into the water.

While Doug and Dad pushed a switch on their reels to let the line down into the water, I was told to manually pull my line. This was about fifty feet of line pulling, I might add. After pulling the line and reeling it in about a *zillion* times, my forearms were screaming. Also, I faintly remember Doug saying something about being careful—reel knob—and blasting your thumb. All this ensured that my enthusiasm, if any, for salmon fishing had vanished. In addition, the waves were so high that when I finally hooked the fish, Dad had to wrap his arms around me to keep me from flying overboard. At this point I must add that catching a big thirty-five-to fifty-pound salmon is a tremendous thrill. You work for it, but it is truly a thrill.

With Doug at the helm and in full destroy Mary Anne mode, there was a chance of the dreaded seasickness problem. As I had once, many years before, become horribly seasick, I was determined to conquer this possibility. Since I was now a fairly new bride and trying to prove to my husband that I could and would enjoy his love of fishing, I prayed and prayed that I would remain in good health. I realize that fishing was becoming a religious experience, as I found myself praying more and more. This, along with a bit of Dramamine and staring at the distant horizon, allowed me to fish right along with the big boys.

Doug finally decided I was not going to go away, so he introduced me to the magical reel switch, which allowed the fishing line to drop with little or no effort. Glory be, I had arrived.

One memorable outing was of my hooking a really good salmon. Trooper that I am, I fought the fish for quite a while before the line suddenly went limp or slack, as we say in fishing lingo. Glancing over to the water's edge, I spied the culprit seal enjoying his dinner at the expense of my fish.

Bamfield is a funny little town. From our cabin we could easily walk to the village, where we could find a café and coffee/ice cream parlor that was never open. Along this blackberry bush pathway, we would stop to use a pay telephone so Dad could call his office. Can you imagine a pay phone booth in the middle of a wooded area? Thank goodness for collect calls. Supplies were brought in by watercraft—some kind of barge, I think. There appeared to be no supply schedule, and groceries were always a surprise when and if they arrived. Such things as bread and milk were treasures. For this reason, Dad and I always rented a car in order to stop along the way for provisions before arriving in Bamfield.

Salmon fishing was great fun for many years. Finally, the fish count began to drop, and the fishing laws became so strict that only one fish per day would be the legal limit. I should add that going fishing and not catching anything for several hours a day puts Dad in a ***VERY BAD MOOD***. So we decided to explore new fishing venues. Before leaving Bamfield, I actually managed to interpret the cabin signs and deposit the refuse in the proper cans—I think. And Doug and I became good friends for the duration of our fishing trips to Bamfield.

Also at this point I should add that we did find a better way to travel to Bamfield without having to wait for the ferry. And sipping tea at the famous and regal Empress Hotel in Victoria, Canada, helped fade the memories of the ferry wait. The Victoria stop was introduced with the onset of the new travel arrangements that allowed us to fly to Canada without taking the ferry. Imagine that!

Ranger Rick and His Flying Machine

Fairbanks, Alaska

One warm and sunny afternoon in Hawaii, while sipping a colorful umbrella drink, Dad began to reminisce about previous fishing trips to Alaska. It turns out Dad knew an old bush pilot who would fly into wilderness areas for lake fishing. This is something Dad thought he would like to do again.

After spending untold hours on the telephone—the Internet was not to be at that time—we located a bush pilot in Fairbanks who had known Dad's previous pilot. The previous pilot was no longer flying. He probably had good sense to be enjoying an umbrella drink somewhere—either Hawaii or Mexico—rather than stuffing tourist fishermen into his small aircraft. Following much discussion, we made arrangements to go to Fairbanks for a few days of wilderness lake fishing. I make this point, for when one tells they're going to Fairbanks for fishing, they are considered *daft,* as Fairbanks is inland Alaska. However, pilot Rick promised to fly us for about forty minutes to land on lakes, where we would find rainbow trout and landlocked salmon.

Ranger Rick, as I would lovingly name him, was as particular as the cabin keepers in Bamfield. Prior to our landing in Fairbanks, he wanted credit card information and how much we weighed. I rarely tell loved ones how much I weigh, much less strange men on the telephone. However, I do reluctantly confess, I may have fudged a pound or two, as I was starting my "diet" the next day.

Ranger Rick reminded us to bring parkas, as it ***could*** be cold on the lakes even though it was August. Rick furnished, for a price, hip boots, little boats with motors, and rods and reels. Sometimes, if he remembered, we would even get a net. He kept no bait available and always reminded us that he was the pilot and not a fishing guide.

Rick flew a single-engine, four-seat airplane that stretched to six seats if the weight allowed for this. As I was an experienced passenger of small aircraft, I had no fear about flying and landing on the lake. Taking off and landing these floatplanes with an experienced pilot at the wheel should be a piece of cake. Well, now let me tell you there is little or no room for error when landing these aircraft. Never have I seen a landing area looks so narrow, so wet, and so small. Also, I learned that if the pilot attempts to slow down too quickly when landing on the water, the plane could nose-dive down, flip over, and go underwater. Underwater to me means I might *DROWN*. For this reason, I recommend that you always fly with a pilot who has gray hair and is very particular about his airplane. Also, their past safe-flying record with lots and lots of flying hours logged is a definite plus. All these good qualities we found in pilot Rick.

Climbing into his aircraft complete with heavy parka and rubber hip boots (which were usually too big) was an almost impossible job. All the while, Rick would be giving orders, such as "don't hang onto that," "don't let your hips rub on the upholstery," "don't use mosquito spray prior to landing the craft at the lake," "don't get your boot mud in the plane," "don't clean the fish on the lake bank, as it will attract bears and more." Rick always asked Dad to sit in the right seat, as Dad once, ***MANY YEARS AGO*** (fifty years or so), had a pilot's license. Rick said this was in case he (Rick) had "the big one," Dad could land the plane. ***WHAT!***

On one occasion, Rick had four air force jet pilots as passengers along with us. The pilots were in complete awe of Rick's ability to maneuver the airplane into and out of such close quarters. In fact, the pilots scheduled another day of fishing just so they could enjoy the flying experience with Rick. I truly enjoyed the pilots, as they referred to me as "ma'am," something I had not heard since I moved from Texas and the South.

Bringing too much gear—i. e., food, ice coolers, bottled beverages, and sleeping bags—resulted in a deep frown and cross words from Rick. Also, passengers who weighed over 250 pounds were occasionally denied the flight. At least Dad and I avoided those problems. That is, as long as we stayed away from the biscuits and gravy at the local family restaurant.

Once during our outing, I got completely drenched with rain—not a dry thread on me. I was afraid Rick would leave me at the lake all night until I dried off. Well, he did let me fly, but I'm sure he was miserable knowing how wet I was getting the backseat. He still reminds me of how very wet I was. A very persnickety man, that Rick.

We fished three different lakes during our annual trips to Fairbanks. And each of these lakes had a cabin or two in which to stay. Dad stayed overnight several times, but I draw the line when there is no running water. At my age, there is usually a trip to the potty at least once during the night. The thought of walking down a path to the outhouse in the night and probably negotiating at some point with a bear was not something I was going to do. And I did not. Dad did.

Rick loved it when Dad chose to stay overnight. Rick wasn't too thrilled about having to make the round trip to pick me up, but what he did like was that Dad traveled light. All Dad needed was a can of spam, fishing bait, and a bottle of water. Rick had sleeping bags in his cabins, and Dad did not seem to care who or what had been in those bags. That, along with the outhouse, sealed the notion of my ever being an overnight guest—no matter how much guilt was put on me. And believe me, there was plenty.

Dad had more than one evening of excitement while staying in Rick's cabins. Once, while sitting on the porch and watching the evening sun (as the sun never sets in the summer in Alaska), Dad began to hear a strange noise. It sounded as if someone might be hammering on the aluminum boats at water's edge. Dad toddled down to the edge of the lake, and lo and behold, what did he find but seagulls pecking on the floor of the boat. Apparently, Dad had left shrimp bait out to dry, and the seagulls thought that Dad had certainly left them a wonderful dinner. I am still amazed that seagulls appeared on a lake in the middle of an Alaskan mountain range.

Another memorable evening, and perhaps the most exciting, was Dad's adventure with a bear. No, he was not on his way to the outhouse but was sleeping soundly in a sleeping bag that evening. Dad heard a rustling noise and looked up to the large picture window of the cabin to see a big black bear standing full mount and peering in. Dad did not know whether to be still, to make a noise, or to hide. He concluded that being still was probably the best choice. The bear looked and looked and probably decided that Dad was not on his dinner menu that night. So off the bear waddled and Dad was once again saved.

Together, Dad and I did experience a rather interesting bear event. While fishing, I apparently hooked a rather large fish. The fish wound round and round the boat and finally took a dive under the boat, which broke my fishing pole in half. Fortunately, we always carry a spare pole and leave it at lakeside. As Dad started to motor us back to the edge of the lake, he said, "Look at the other fishing boat. There is a bear sitting in the boat." As we got closer to the boat, the bear became frightened, jumped out, and wandered up the hill. As we neared waters edge, Dad said, "Get out and go get your fishing pole." I exclaimed, "You want me to get out of this boat and get near the bear?" I did not get out of the boat and Dad did. As I have previously said, I do not do bears. I do not know if this exercise confirmed Dad's love of fishing or if it proclaimed his love for me. I would like to think it was a bit of both.

There is a certain beauty on wilderness lakes that is touched by few. For the most part, the water is usually calm, the sky blue, and the only sound might be the song of a loon. Ducks swim along with their flock of ducklings following. Once we saw a mother duck with her family of thirteen ducklings paddling behind like little soldiers. She was having a terrible time keeping them all in line. There always seemed to be at least three or four floating off in different directions. Bald eagles fly frequently overhead, hoping to swoop down on an unsuspecting fish for their dinner. Drowsy mother bears, fresh from hibernation, and their newly born cubs wade the water's edge looking for their fish supper. And mother moose walk along with their one or two babies, on unstable legs, trying desperately to keep up. Mother moose go at a brisk pace and expect their young to stay close by. I suppose this is their way of teaching them how to discourage predators.

You sure don't want to tangle with the mother moose. Once we were fishing just offshore when a mother moose decided we were a bit too close to her baby. Mom moose turned and began to charge toward the boat. I yelled, "Start the motor and let's get out of here." We did escape but she was one angry moose. I hear that attacks by moose are the leading cause of accidental death in Alaska. I don't know if this is true, but it seems plausible to me.

The fishing lakes were surrounded by cabins that were lifesavers during afternoon rainstorms. One especially nice cabin always had its screen door unlocked, and the porch served as a haven for us more than once. Here, I must say this cabin also had no running water and required a ladder in order to climb up to the sleeping loft. Ladders are not good things for folks over the age of about forty-five. One cabin had a rather festive owner—a female, I might add. She would pilot her plane in for a day or two of weekend frolic and little or no fishing. One of her favorite things to do, along with her guests, would be to *moon* the fisherman on the lake. This was solely for the thrill of shock but all in good fun.

The town of Fairbanks is a sleepy little town, except for the new mall areas down by the freeway. Dad especially loves the old downtown area. I think he would like to spend considerable time in Fairbanks if it were not for the extreme cold weather in the winter. Even Ranger Rick goes to warmer weather for the winter season. Fairbanks does not get as much snow as Anchorage, but the temperature is much colder. On one winter day, the high temperature was—30°.

The summer flowers in Fairbanks are magnificent, with their blooms vibrant with color. As it is almost twenty-four hours of daylight in the summer, the flowers grow profusely. It seems we are usually there during lilac-blooming season, as whole areas are alive with their fragrance. We often sneak a blossom or two to bring to our hotel room to enjoy.

Occasionally, we would take a day off from fishing to drive around the area. Just a short distance up the road is North Pole, Alaska. There you will find a large building with Merry Christmas signs painted on the walls. Inside you can find almost every Christmas decoration known to man. Outside, in a fenced area, there are reindeer resting up from their frantic Christmas Eve night. I looked but did not see Rudolph, or maybe his red nose bulb had just burned out. It is from this exact North Pole that letters to Santa are answered. It's good to see that Santa has so many helpers.

There Are No Fleas in This Market

Anchorage, Alaska

In addition to our love of Fairbanks, we have grown fond of Anchorage. In the beginning, our trips to Alaska began and ended in Anchorage, as air transportation was more plentiful there. Nowadays, we try to plan our trips so as to include a day or two in Anchorage at the Holiday Inn Express near the airport. Dad really enjoys their biscuits and gravy there. (Don't forget that food is one of the four *F*s mentioned previously.)

Downtown Anchorage has grown into quite a nice city, with office buildings and shopping malls housing Nordstrom's, Penney's, and Macy's. Also there are major hotel chains such as Hilton and Sheraton, to name just a few. Of course Main Street has its share of souvenir T-shirt shops that also peddle the usual key chains and coffee mugs. By the way, this is the same street that is the starting point of the famous Iditarod dog run. They chase right through downtown Anchorage, ending the race in Nome. I felt better when I learned the dogs wear little shoes.

One of our favorite things in Anchorage is the weekend flea market. There you will find clothing, produce, food of all sorts, crafts, and more. Salmon and halibut treats abound. You will find everything from grilled fish, fried fish and chips, and fish tacos, my all-time favorite. And if you have room for dessert, the aromatic waft of funnel cakes frying will tempt you beyond belief. Beautiful produce is plentiful, with strawberries, tomatoes, squash, peaches, and melons waiting for purchase. After visiting with one vendor, we discovered that all his produce came from California. It was interesting that none of this fresh produce was available to us in California at that time. Now I know where it goes—to Alaska. Our stuff comes from Chile.

We found one lovely craft lady to be especially entrepreneurial. She made and painted, quite handsomely, wooden ties the style a businessman might wear. She was especially proud of the fact the ties were hinged at regular intervals so they could be folded, if necessary. The following year when we visited the market, we did not see her. We hoped she had sold out of ties and had gone home to enjoy the wealth of her work. However, it would take a special customer to find the need for wooden ties, even though I suppose they would last a lifetime.

As Dad and I were a bit stiff from our five days of fishing in a small boat for seven hours a stretch, we thought we had found Mecca when we spied a booth boasting of upper-body massage therapy. There, two petite Asian women promised to make us feel good as new. Dad, being particularly generous, suggested we each take part in this adventure. With our straddling two forward-leaning half tables and placing our heads on some sort of headrest, the therapist began their own brand of personal torture. Never have I experienced such tiny fingers doing such damage to my body. The twenty-minute procedure seemed like an eternity. As Dad was so kind to share this with me, I dared not complain about the pain. It was later I learned he was experiencing the same amount of agony as I. In conclusion, beware of tiny Asian women with strong pointy fingers. Now that I think about it, I suspect they left their fingerprints in the form of bruises so that they might be charged with a felony assault. Just kidding—not about the bruises!

Combat Fishing in Luxury

Kenai, Alaska

After several trips to our Fairbanks fishing paradise, we decided to explore the Kenai Peninsula. Friends had given us reports of good fishing and campgrounds in the area. It was there I found my favorite style of camping out in a cabin. Our cabin was part of a rather luxurious lodge with a four-star restaurant. The cabin had a sitting room with a wood stove, a king-size bed, television, bar, and full bathroom. It was nestled among the pine trees with a view of a snowcapped mountain. The entire lodge followed along the banks of the gorgeous turquoise Kenai River. Oh yes, this is Mom's kind of camping. I am told that during salmon-fishing season on the river, there are so many shoulder-to-shoulder fishermen that it is called *combat* fishing. But for Dad and me, we'll settle for the quiet and calm lake fishing. Just wish I could take the cabin with me.

While in the area, Dad and I spotted a diner that also boasted of having access to a fly-in-fishing pilot. Well, what can I say! Remember the previously mentioned *F*? We began the search in hot pursuit. Finding the pilot, we believed him to be well qualified, along with a sturdy airplane. At least he had the required gray hair. The pilot said he could fly us to a wilderness lake where fine trout could be caught. Of course, said he, if the weather happened to turn bad—i.e., heavy rain, wind, etc.—he would have to leave us there until the weather cleared. This might be for two or three days. ***SAY WHAT!***

As there was no shelter by the lake—not even a bear-infested cabin with no running water—we decided that we best be on our way to visit Seward and the luxury of another Holiday Inn Express. Don't forget, their biscuits and gravy are good.

Halibut Is King

Seward, Alaska

One really fun trip in easy driving distance from Anchorage is Seward, which is a quaint town on the coast. Fishing, both charter and commercial, is the main commodity there. As far as I am concerned, all halibut begins and ends in Seward. It is worth *breaking training* to dine on the local fish and chips. At a somewhat greasy spoon, one will find the most delicious halibut and chips. As we have traveled to Seward several times, we always find our way to our favorite fish and chips diner. One can watch the halibut being taken from the fishing boats across the street and brought to the diner. Actually this has ruined us for eating halibut anywhere else in the world.

Seward is one of my favorite Alaska towns. The downtown area probably has not changed much since it was rebuilt following the tragic earthquake in the 1900s. There is a wonderful store that sells heavy clothing to keep the citizens warm. Also, the store boasts a superb collection of Hately socks and T-shirts. The sox usually sport bear paw prints or reindeer silhouettes. The T-shirts have great sayings of wisdom, such as "take a hike" under a picture of a beaver with a backpack walking down a trail. This one I wanted to purchase for a one-time girlfriend of our son. Dad said it would not be in good taste. The girlfriend finally did *take a hike* and without the encouragement of the T-shirt. Thank goodness for that.

Seward weather in June can be somewhat chancy. Once we tried to schedule a fishing trip, but the wind kept the boats in dock.

One of my fantasies is to purchase a fishing license, pay for the fishing trip, and give it all to someone who would then go out and catch fish for me. As of yet this has not happened. By way for a taste of history, Alaska was purchased from Russia in 1867 by a man named William H Seward. This purchase became known as Seward's Folly. William Seward was secretary of state under President Abraham Lincoln. There still is a good bit of Russian influence in Alaska in their onion-topped churches and artwork. In 1960, a 9.6 earthquake shook Alaska with the epicenter just a short way from Seward. Anchorage suffered mass destruction, and Seward was almost completely destroyed as well.

After stuffing our bodies with halibut and biscuits and gravy, we decided to waddle our way on to Homer to explore the spit and the home of notorious fishing.

Battle on the Spit

Homer, Alaska

Dad has a genius client who once told him that he and his wife would like to retire to Homer. Well, that was good enough for us to commence our exploration of the Homer Spit. We only spent two nights in Homer. First of all, the well-known motel chain where we had made reservations was surely less than we expected. No television in working order along with no computer capability. Those are bad words for Dad. Also, there was the threat of possibly no telephone service and certainly no biscuits and gravy.

After finding alternate accommodations, we decided to give Homer a fair look. We found a local diner with rather good fare. Down on the spit, we found an acceptable fish and chips respite, not in the league of Seward, I might add, but adequate. As we sampled our fish and chips by the waterfront, a dark gray cloud shaded the sun. There we witnessed a most violent windstorm capture the area. Fishing boats of all sizes tossed and turned, with water crashing over their bows. Boat captains attempted to stay upright while fighting for their crafts to make land. As you might imagine, Dad and I did not think fishing in Homer was the thing for us.

I began to wonder if Dad's genius client had ever actually been in Homer when one of these weather spectacles occurred. I don't know. What I do know is that he retired on an island in Puget Sound, Washington. At this point, I might add that he also had considered retirement in Nashville, Tennessee, without ever having been there. Later, while attending a business meeting in Nashville with Dad, genius client determined the heat and humidity might "do him in" for good, so Nashville was deleted from the list of his retirement havens. See, I told you he was a genius.

Having explored Alaska's coastline and back roads for several years, we determined our wilderness lake fishing with Ranger Rick best suited us in our advanced age. We still go there annually and always will, as long as we don't eat too many biscuits and gravy and miss the airplane weight limit and as long as Rick can help push and stuff us in the small confines of his airplane *without our touching anything.*

Fishing is still fun and life is good!

PART II

Europe

Europe

Europe is a trip Dad has made annually for many years—way before I came into the picture. Initially, it was done just before or the day after Christmas. As Dad is not a Christmas person, it was his way of escaping the frantic pace of the holidays. But as a Mom, I am a Christmas person, and Dad's holiday panic changed dramatically upon my arrival into his life. Oh, I believe the panic is still there, but my holiday spirit has seeped little by little into his being. We have a Christmas tree, gifts, music, Christmas Eve church, and Dad's all-time favorite, turkey and dressing. There is that *F* again. We don't go to Europe at Christmastime anymore but I will explain that later.

As I enter into sharing this phase of life with Dad, I should like to give a bit of my prior travel background. My first time to visit Europe was to Paris. I experienced Paris almost like no one can expect to do. This was accomplished by the fact of my being included in an exclusive group of American business presidents. We were treated to private shows of haute couture by famous fashion designers and a tour of the shop of Hermes, where the leather on a handbag felt as soft as a baby's bottom. The dream of owning the buttery leather handbag, with the dashing gold *H* on its side, was a longtime fantasy of mine. By the way, I had tithed portions of my savings for several months just to purchase such a handbag from Hermes. However, when it got down to the time of decision, I refused to pay the price. But I still think about it many years later.

Moving on, there was a private tour of the Orsay Museum. Impressionism is my favorite period of art—van Gogh, Renoir, and Degas, to name a few. Not too much Monet, as I quickly tire of all those water lilies. One delicious dinner was held in a large restored area of the Conciergerie, the guillotine, where Marie Antoinette was imprisoned and beheaded. It was there I sampled a most delicious first course, which was of pâté consistency. After returning home, I spent many hours in bookstores attempting to research the ingredients of the pâté (written in French on the individual menus) so that I might try to prepare it. I must say I was terribly shocked to finally learn I had eaten and enjoyed EEL.

To top it all, there was a formal dinner in the hall of mirrors in the Palace of Versailles, with a spectacular fireworks display for evenings end entertainment. Our waiter, who served our entrée of cold chicken (as there is no hot kitchen in the palace), asked me what group we were, as a dinner party of this magnitude is usually given only for visiting presidents, prime ministers, and royalty.

Of course it is "only by accident of birth that I am not royalty" (a favorite quote of mine from a wonderful British actress named Patricia Rutledge).

My second trip to Europe was made with my good friend Ida Jo. Ida appeared at my front door one evening waving a brochure from our country club, announcing a tour of Spain and Portugal. We decided the price was right, and certainly the country club members would be more than acceptable traveling companions—snobs that we were.

Visiting Spain and Portugal with Ida was delightful even though it included some tour bus travel—UGH. It was everything we expected. There was paella for dinner, pearls in Majorca, and the Alcazar, where Queen Isabella reputedly told Columbus he could have the money to go exploring—and we all know how that ended.

Then Ida explained the biggest expense of the trip was, of course, the airfare. She suggested that while we were in Europe, the two of us should visit more countries. And so we did. With Victor, who was Austrian and only spoke German, as our private driver, we toured Germany, Austria, and a bit of Switzerland. Ida's description of Victor was that he looked like Sean Connery with bad teeth. She was pretty much on target. Victor drove us to every castle and most museums in the country. He bought tapes for the radio I think just to shut us up. We listened to the likes of Tom Jones, Ida's favorite, and Diana Ross, my favorite, for hours on end.

He wheeled us over the Swiss Alps while Ida and I took a sip of CC and scotch straight from the bottles, as it was also time for Ida to take her blood pressure medicine, which required liquid to down the pill, and that was all there was to drink.

In Vienna, Victor was pleased to take us to dinner at a "*world-famous*" Wiener schnitzel eatery. We were seated outside on a patio when I heard the familiar thump of the disco beat, my favorite music at the time—and sort of still is. I asked where the disco was as I thought that might be a good addition to the evening's festivities. From time to time Ida and I had been crowned, in private circles, the disco duck and the prima ballerina. Well, friends, that drumbeat turned out to be the kitchen cooks pounding the pork for the schnitzel. Even though a tad embarrassed, I managed to woof down my dinner, finishing it off with warm apple strudel and ice cream.

Every day, Victor would say we were going to "make many steps." This meant that we were going to walk at least one hundred miles while Victor napped in the car. This was okay in that all the schnitzel and strudel melted away fifteen pounds. I share all of this with you only that you should know that these experiences, no matter how privileged, pale like a total lunar eclipse in comparison to my adventures with Dad. Yes, Dad and I traveled in lots of European countries, and those stories will be given to you down the road a bit. But first we must visit Germany, as that is where our European adventures began.

Germany

Having stood the ground on my not wanting to be away from home on Christmas Day, Dad and I compromised by flying to Germany the day after. This was truly an adventure for me, as Dad and I had been married only a short six months, and we were still getting to know one another.

First of all, one should be very careful when eating airline food that has been prepared for Christmas Day consumption and then served again the following day. This was presumed to be so, in that the fare consisted of red and green pasta of unknown origin—an absolute gastronomic train wreck. The gods were with us in that we remained in rather good health even after a generous sampling of the somewhat colorful and mysterious meal.

After an all-night flight, in the back of the bus so to speak, we unwound ourselves enough to deplane in frigid Frankfurt, Germany. Gathering our belongings, we staggered our way to the rental car agency. This is where we rented a Fiat, tiny in stature and of undisclosed semi-antique vintage. The engine was at least "first cousin" to our washing machine left behind in California. (I feared the washing machine might be more reliable.)

Unbeknownst to me, Dad had a grand plan of winding our way down the Romantik Road in Bavaria to Rothenburg ob der Tauber. As a clue of things to come, then and for our future travels, we took a left turn out of the airport toward Cologne. After not too many miles, or kilometers I should say, Dad professed we were going the wrong way. It proved to be the beginning of a familiar lament: "*I think we are lost again.*"

Schneeballen, a Major Food Group

Rothenburg ob der Tauber

When Dad and I began our initial discussion regarding travel plans, including lodging, he explained to me that he never made advance reservations for a night's stay. Of course, this terrified me in that previously I always knew my daily travel route and where I would put my head at night. He also shared with me the fact *that some hotels on the edge of town were better than others*. Previously, Dad had stayed in local *gasthauses* in the countryside. There he would sleep under fluffy down comforters and share breakfast with the host family. Dad's eyes still get misty when he reminisces about freshly baked bread, cold cuts, cheese, and pure German butter. (Remember the *F*s)

My fear of a *gasthaus* was that there might not be a private bathroom. So I stated the claim that my minimum requirements for lodging included a private bathroom, preferably with a bathtub, and a clean room. Also, it helps if the window coverings are attached firmly to the wall and not sagging downward. I was soon to learn that "clean" is not a problem in Germany. The Germans maintain a tidy culture. Even their firewood is cut in specific links and is stacked perfectly outside their homes. This is somewhat different from the French and Spanish, where their firewood appears to have survived an explosion of massive force.

Having arrived in Frankfurt, making a wrong turn and righting ourselves by way of a sharp U-turn, we were finally on our way to Rothenburg. Driving the autobahn was certainly thrilling as autos flew past us at Mach 1 speed. Our little Fiat, with its engine wound as tightly as possible, was no match for the big German Mercedes Benz, BMWs, and Porches, which always seemed to be snapping at our *tail feathers.*

A personal observation of mine was that I rarely saw physically challenged people. I believe it is because when there is an automobile accident traveling at the speed of light, the occupants are probably killed and not just injured. This mental vision did not help my driving confidence very much. The good news was that the speedometers are calibrated in kilometers, instead of miles per hour, and thus I had no idea just how fast Dad was going. To be fair, I must say I have never seen an auto accident on the autobahn. The Germans are extremely good drivers. I don't remember seeing any old cars either, but there always seems to be an ample supply of old people.

Screaming down the autobahn as fast as our little Fiat could scream, we quickly reached our destination, Rothenburg. I was grateful for this, as my lack of sleep on the thirteen-hour airplane flight, plus a nine-hour time change, had me in a staggering mode. The bitter cold was not much of a help either. In fact, I have heard that when freezing to death, one goes to sleep just before they die.

Being the ever-considerate husband, Dad asked where I might like to stay. Here I was cross-eyed from exhaustion, partially frozen, and had no idea of where I was. But I still managed to spot a small hotel that (hopefully) would suit our needs. The innkeeper graciously walked us up two flights of stairs to see the available room. There it was, Mecca, or so I thought. The beds had huge fluffy down comforters, a tiny round table with linen cloth, one elf-size chair, and—ta-da (drumroll)—a bathroom with potty and shower. Somehow, the German-speaking innkeeper and

English-only-speaking Dad came to an arrangement, and the room became ours for the night.

The first order of business was to take a potty break, followed by a short nap under the warm comforter. It was then I discovered the bathroom had been converted from possibly a tiny broom closet. In order to accomplish potty duties, one had to sit sidesaddle on the toilet. As most people have knees, it was impossible to close the door in any seated position. Squeezing sideways into the shower presented another set of challenges. The small amount of personal modesty I coveted quickly vanished. But potty break and nap it was to be. After a few hours, we felt we should wander downstairs and find the origin of the delicious-smelling food. And there it was, two small dining rooms—one for the local Germans and one for us. We felt a bit like a curiosity for the local tribe.

At this point, we learned two very important things that would help us in Germany for years and years to come. The first being that if a menu is written in German and no one around speaks English, you are always safe in ordering Wiener schnitzel. Folks, that is old chicken fried steak without gravy (pork) in any language.

The second is a wine lesson. German red wine, my beverage of choice, is good wine. They rarely use terms such as "cabernet," "merlot," etc. In most cases they say red wine dry, medium, or sweet. As my basic nature is not to be extreme, I always order *medium*. German red wine is not exported to the United States, as I understand it does not travel well. The same goes for their delicious cold-cut meats.

My favorite medium red wine is Trollinger. This name was given to me by English-speaking waiters. I since have learned that Trollinger is actually a grape from the Trocken region. At any rate, my medium red Trollinger can be found anywhere from Kool-Aid pink to dark burgundy red. It tastes a bit like California rose and goes well with Wiener schnitzel.

I'm certain the Trollinger alcohol content is very low, as it has never made the tip of my nose tingle. Also, it is best served in the local Roemer wineglass, which has a clear round bowl and a thick green stem and base. The latest models even have grapevines etched around the bowls. After many weeks of searching for these glasses, I found they could be purchased from Woolworth's in Munich—which I did. By the way, the cashiers at Woolworth's are very helpful and honest. Most speak no English, and as I speak no German, the basic exchange of currency for goods can be difficult. But I solved this as well. I simply put a wad of German currency in my hand, show it to the cashier, and she takes out what I guess to be the proper amount. For future reference, in addition to the Roemer wineglasses, Woolworth's also has a good variety of fingernail glue in case of an emergency.

Finishing our Wiener schnitzel and medium wine, Dad suggested a walk inside the walled city. First of all, it was bloody cold, and I had no idea what or where the walled city was about. But being a good sport and also remembering that our room had only one elf chair for sitting, I decided it was probably a fine idea.

Rothenburg is the best preserved city in Europe. Its walls date back to the thirteenth century. Rothenburg Castle was built in 1142 on the mountain high above the river Tauber. In 1356, the castle was destroyed; however, the castle gardens still remain. In 1170, the city of Rothenburg was founded. Rothenburg is a medieval city with characteristic Bavarian architecture and charm.

While finally putting our "staggers" aside for the moment and bundling up to resemble *Michelin Men* on parade, we made our first journey inside the walled city. And to add to the evening delight, the winter snow began to gently fall. We wandered up to a large window and looked through to see the most endearing sight. There in the dining room was a man playing the zither with his young daughter, about eight years old, singing "Silent Night." This began my love affair with Rothenburg that remains to this day. Snow was falling, music was playing, white lights twinkled, and colorful decorations sparkled. At that point, I told Dad if we ever spent Christmas day away from home, I would like for it to be in Rothenburg. And years later this happened. By the way, that dining area was part of a lovely old hotel, the Hotel Markstrum. The hotel was originally built in 1264 as a customs house. It became our home for all future visits to Rothenburg.

Shuffling our way back to the hotel, spare in comparison to the Markstrum, we decided we should go to bed before we completely dropped. After dealing with the sidesaddle potty and challenging shower, we flopped in a most wonderful bed.

At this point, I should tell you that one of my Christmas stocking gifts from Dad was a pair of Rudolph-motif woolly socks, which, when pressed firmly on the side, played "Rudolph the Red-Nosed Reindeer." I brought these lovely fashion statements along instead of house slippers, as they took up little space in my suitcase. When getting up in the night to negotiate with the potty, I stepped on the socks, which began to play, rather loudly, "Rudolph the Red-Nosed Reindeer." This music was for all the hotel guests to hear, as our bedroom walls were paper thin. Also, it didn't help that Dad and I broke into wails of laughter. We still wonder what the German guests must have thought was going on in the room with the giddy American couple.

Next morning, following a traditional German breakfast of sliced cheese, cold cuts, and dark grain bread, we decided to explore inside the walled city in the light of day. This breakfast menu was hard for me to understand in that Dad's favorite breakfast at home is "one more pancake and hash brown potatoes, please." And as usual, I was still looking for scrambled eggs with salsa.

Again, heavily wrapped to protect us from the bitter cold, we began our walk. The absolute charm of this wonderful Bavarian city warmed us so that the frigid temperature was soon forgotten.

There were flower shops aplenty, as the Germans do love their flowers. Also, the shops are called *Blumen*. Wonderful name, I think. There was a shop that sold Lyke houses. These are ceramic houses of different Bavarian styles that hold tea lights inside to show lights gleaming through the windows. I loved these houses and began a collection.

We found butcher shops, produce shops, "stuff for tourists" shops—and then there it was, in the front window of a confectionery was a pastry ball about the size of a softball. These balls were woven into a sphere from leftover pastry, pie crust in texture. There were chocolate covered balls, powdered-sugar balls, caramel-coated balls, cinnamon/sugar balls, and more. The *Schneeballen,* English translated "snowballs," are unique to Rothenburg, and I had to have one—or maybe two.

Now I ask you, have your jeans ever gotten so tight that if you put your cell phone in your hip pocket you might dial someone in, say, New Zealand? Or have you ever put your car keys in your side pocket and set off the car alarm? Well, I just want you to understand about my muffin-top body.

Do you actually think that was a deterrent to the purchasing and inhaling said *snowball*? Well, it was not, and I would do it again tomorrow if the opportunity occurred. Some folks describe the *Schneeballen* as bland pie strips rolled into a ball and covered with some sort of glop. Obviously, they don't know fine gourmet pastry as ole muffin top does. Also, it occurred to me that this was one kind of souvenir that I could eat and not have to take through customs on our way home to the United States. That is unless the TSA body image machine exposed a large lump, of undetermined density, lodged somewhere in my abdominal cavity. Well, actually, I did take it through customs but in the form of an increased double muffin top.

In addition to the unforgiving *Schneeballen*, there is the large soft pretzel. This delectable piece of dough is, I am certain, one of the seven major food groups and should be eaten daily—in numbers. These pretzels are everywhere. They are in pastry shops, beer gardens, stubes, and airports, to name a few. In eateries, they are placed on the table without having to ask. In fact, they might be the national food of Germany, like Spam is for Hawaii. And needless to say, I love them. Another major food group is sausage and sauerkraut. You will find bratwurst, knockwurst, Nürnburg sausages, and more. These are served with sauerkraut, which has become my gold standard for all German food; for Dad, roasted potatoes are the standard.

Just off the *Marktplatz* (market square) is a restaurant that appeared to cater to the local folks. Here I found my Nürnberg sausages and sauerkraut, Dad's roasted potatoes, a series of scrumptious soups, and, of course, the obligatory pretzels. Our first trip there was for an early dinner. We dined at a meandering pace, savoring each course along with an appropriate wine (Trollinger, of course) and coffee. When presented with the check, we were surprised to learn it was a CASH ONLY restaurant. Dad began fingering through his wallet, looking for the needed funds. When he started frantically digging in his pockets, I became somewhat panicked. As I had enjoyed an afternoon of shopping, I was not too sure I had any money either. We had absolutely no idea what happened to persons who could not pay their bill. *Perhaps jail or even worse.* As we had recently visited the Rothenburg Torture Museum, all sorts of visions came to mind. As I searched through my handbag, which thankfully I had brought with me as often I do not, I found just enough coins to help pay the bill. Don't get me wrong, every time we are in Rothenburg we go back there for a meal or two; we just remember to take cash money.

Now changing directions for a moment, I should like to give you a bit of my early background. A great deal of my life was spent within an approximate three-mile radius—my home as a child, my schools, my church, and, later in years, my married home and country club. As you can surmise, I never needed a driving map. In later years, my long-distance driving consisted of Houston to Vail, Colorado, which I did fairly often and knew by memory. Again, no map needed.

When Dad and I married and began our European adventures, a map was a necessity. My task was to read and use the map to get us from one foreign country to another. Our first year of adventure found us accidentally in Switzerland, instead of Germany—twice in the space of one hour. This was my first attempt at map navigation. In my never-give-up mode, I was determined to navigate us from Munich to Rothenburg, making no wrong turns and using a map for guidance.

My well-traveled friend, Jimi, and I were having lunch one day when I told her how Dad and I love Rothenburg. She agreed. I did notice she pronounced "Rothenburg" as "**ROTTENBERG**." From that day forward I began pronouncing the double *t*s as opposed to the *th*. Jimi had traveled more than I, which made me certain her pronunciation was the correct one.

So back to our driving trip to Rottenburg. Off we go, Munich to Rothenburg. Yes, siree, no wrong turns; road signs agreed with the map, and lo and behold (drumroll, please) we arrived at our destination. Yes, I was ready for my victory dance. Finding a parking space, we walked into the old city, which looked vaguely familiar but a bit strange as well. Perhaps we entered through a different gate? Following a potty stop and coffee break, we walked outside only to see a large city directory and map. And there it was, ROTTENBURG AM NECKAR. I had managed to *precisely*—now don't forget the word "precisely"—deliver us to the wrong city. We were looking to arrive at Rothenburg ob der Tauber. I'm not sure there is a moral to this story—only that the driving map was wrestled away from me never to be returned for the duration of the trip. I really am not a complete dumbbell, as I did master a GPS system with German audio instructions. Now I am a self-proclaimed electronic genius. I just don't do maps.

Armed with a chocolate-covered *Schneeballen*, a ceramic Lyke church house, and a stuffed schnauzer dog wearing lederhosen and a hat with feather, we began to make our way to our next destination, Garmisch-Partenkirchen.

No Room at the Inn

Garmisch-Partenkirchen

Having spent two days in Rothenburg ob der Tauber, Dad decided it was time to move on down the autobahn to Garmisch-Partenkirchen.

As a bit of history, Partenkirchen originated as a Roman town on the trade route from Venice to Augsburg and is first noted in the year 15 AD. Garmisch is first mentioned some eight hundred years later, suggesting that at some point a Teutonic tribe took up settlement. Garmisch and Partenkirchen remained separate until their respective mayors were forced, by Adolph Hitler, to combine the two market towns in 1935 in anticipation of the 1936 Winter Olympic Games. There is a slightly more modern feel to Garmisch while the cobblestone streets of Partenkirchen offer a glimpse into times past.

Once again, winding up our little Fiat, whom we lovingly called FLASH as a name of encouragement, we streaked our way to Garmisch. As this was my birthday, and the first Dad and I had spent together, it became apparent that Dad wanted to find a special hotel in which to celebrate. And there it was. Just to the right on the outskirts of Garmisch in a grove of tall pine trees was a beautiful multistory hotel of mansion proportion, yellow in color and trimmed in white with flowery market umbrellas dancing in the breeze. Now I'm not sure what all those market umbrellas were doing outside, as the aforementioned breeze was in actuality a BITTER, COLD WIND (to be discussed a bit later). Needless to say, the weather was certainly not conducive to outdoor sitting.

I shall take liberty, again, to digress a bit. Prior to Mom, Dad's European adventures consisted of getting off an airplane, checking the weather forecast, renting a car, and turning in the direction where the weather seemed to be sunny and warm—usually on the coast of something or other. It never occurred to Dad to make advance hotel reservations, as he was never certain where he was going. Kind of reminds me of one of my all-time favorite inspirers of the English language, Yogi Berra, who said something like, "How do you know where you're going if you don't know where you've been?"

But back to Garmisch. The light of reason never shined on the fact that this was December, the peak of the winter ski season and two days before New Year's Eve.

Our little Fiat fishtailed its way up the ice-covered driveway to the lovely yellow mansion-style hotel where Flash did a perfect spinning stop. I remind you that I once lived in Vail, Colorado, and was somewhat used to snow and ice driving. However, I had never experienced such a magnificent twirl as Dad and Flash performed on ice at that moment. This action exceeded any stunt-driver thrill I had ever witnessed in any movie.

Rebundling our half-frozen bodies, we trudged into said hotel seeking a room for a night or two. Don't forget this is the holiday ski season. The proper hotel clerk asked for our reservation confirmation. Uh-oh! Red flags aplenty! I think there may be a bit of larceny running through the veins of some lawyers, as Dad replied—with a big toothy smile—my secretary takes care of that sort of thing and usually by *FAX.* "Well, sir," the clerk replied, "in that case the hotel should have a record of the confirmation." And dear ole Dad proclaimed, "I'm sure you will find it somewhere, as it must have been misplaced." More red flags waving!

At this point I should like to share a story with you that happened many years ago when I was seventeen years old. There seemed to be an obligatory driving trip that most Texans took from Texas to California and usually lasted about two weeks. This vacation, of sorts, was popular in the 1950s. Usual stops were Las Vegas, Grand Canyon, Carmel, Hollywood, Los Angeles, and San Francisco, to name a few. Also, no hotel reservations were usually required or necessary. The vacation included my mom, my friend Sally, and her mom. All went well until we got to San Francisco. We steered our way on to the driveway of the luxurious Fairmont Hotel, parked our shiny new Buick, and sashayed in to request rooms for a night or two. Guess what? "No room at the inn." It was then my mom went into action. Mom explained she was the secretary to the mayor of Houston and he—said mayor—told us he was certain the hotel would accommodate us since we were there on the mayor's behalf.

First of all my mom was NOT the secretary to the mayor—her best friend, Mary Frances, was—and surely we were NOT there on behalf of the mayor or anybody else for that matter. We were there to see THE BRIDGE, eat crab at Fisherman's Wharf, and visit Chinatown.

Perfect as I am, I do have one character flaw and that is I do not and cannot lie. Dad says I am truthful to a fault. As far as I've ever gone is telling a hotel desk clerk he looked like General Dwight Eisenhower, who was running for president at the time. This story gave us a room in Santa Barbara during a SOLD-OUT Fiesta Week. By the way, the hotel clerk did look like General Eisenhower. Well, Mom's award-winning performance resulted in our claiming a two-bedroom suite, at no charge, including an invitation to return any time we wished.

So here in Garmisch I was thinking this must be what Dad had in mind while attempting to snatch a room. Back and forth Dad and the clerk volleyed until the clerk apologetically claimed that there was one tiny room available. This room was usually taken by personal maids or nannies. If we didn't mind that the room was on the first floor and rather small, we could have it for the night. Well, there you go. Dad hit a grand slam. We were given a warm, cozy, and perfectly delightful room in which to spend my birthday. I suppose a little larceny works from time to time.

Having dragged and organized our belongings, we decided it was time to go to the village of Garmisch. Winding up Flash, off we went to explore mostly eateries, as it was well into the afternoon. Spotting a charming hotel, which we later learned was a sister or at least a cousin to the Markstrum in Rothenburg, we agreed to track the delicious aroma wafting through the dining area. Making our way through the glass-enclosed dining cafe/Weinstube, we were seated at what surely was an open patio during the summer months. Glancing upward, we realized we were facing Germany's fourth highest mountain, the Leutasch Dreitorspitze (Three-Gate Peak). The dining area was teeming with boisterous and joyful skiers in their apres-ski mode, telling daring ski stories further motivated by a snifter or two of schnapps. Now Dad and I enjoy a bit of schnapps, but we were in major hunger attention, so sausage and sauerkraut it was to be. And that, my friends, is when and where my "gold standard" was established. Sausage, sauerkraut, apple strudel, and a cup of hot chocolate was the finest birthday lunch of which I could ever dream.

At this point. I must share with you my concern about the German sense of reason and well-being. As I have previously said, it was ***BLOODY HELL COLD*** outside. In fact, Dad and I had never been colder in our lives—even in Colorado. But these skiers had been out of doors and up the fourth highest mountain in Germany for most of the day and had lived to tell the story. I am of German heritage, but I am nowhere or ever have been in that class of German sturdiness. Those folks are *muy fuerte*. Sorry about that! Spanish is my second language and I don't know any German. It's a strange thing that when I am in a foreign country and do not know the language, I have the urge to use Spanish for my communication link. Now how dumb is that? Oops, I've strayed again. Back to Garmisch.

Leaving our haven of warmth and sustenance and believing we would live to tell the story, we once again collided with the brutal cold and wind. As Dad was eager to find a restaurant worthy of my birthday dinner celebration, we began our quest through the village on foot. DON'T FORGET THE COLD. Survival became the urgent need. To accomplish a degree of warmth, we entered one shop, only to leave and enter the shop next door, thus inchworming our way down the *strasse* (street)—there's my German for you. Our longest "layover" was in a bookstore where we pretended to shop for books, which were all written in German. After finding a proper restaurant to reserve for the evening birthday festivity, we began the race back to our friend Fiat Flash. Flash, up to her usual spins and twirls, eventually delivered us safely to the loving arms of our larceny-begotten hotel room. Once inside, we began to thaw, and eventually a feeling returned to our feet and hands. We did count to be sure that all fingers and toes were intact.

As we had put Flash to bed, so to speak, we decided it would be INSANE to get her revved up again to go out for dinner—and of course we were thinking only about Flash. So the birthday dinner was to be in the warmth of our hotel. We learned the formal dining room was completely booked for the night and were invited to dine in the hotel stube. The Gods were with us in that we could not have picked a better spot in all of Garmisch for a birthday dinner.

I don't remember the menu—probably Wiener schnitzel followed by a small snifter of apricot brandy—but I do remember the music and ambiance. The soft romantic music was played on a zither. I wonder if I have a thing for zither people, as this was my second zither sighting in a week. The room was dark wood with burgundy accents, furnished in Bavarian style. There we found a wedding dinner being served to a beautiful mature couple and their family and friends. The bride with flowers in her hair was glowing, and the groom was flushed with pride. All of this combined gave me a delightful and memorable birthday dinner.

The following morning we begrudgingly vacated our ill-begotten room and made plans to move on toward the Mediterranean coastline, where Dad assured me we would find warmth and sunshine. Once again, dragging our luggage out the door, I awaited the arrival of Dad and Flash. Folks, if one thought it was cold yesterday, it was even more frigid that morning. Poor Flash! She had spent the night in an uncovered parking spot and wore a dress heavy with ice crystals. Stuffing our luggage in the miniature trunk, Dad proceeded to give Flash a love pat on the dashboard and turn the key. *VOILA!* After one minor cough, Flash cranked right up, made one last spin, and said, "Let's get to warmer climate." And so we did.

This concluded my initial trip to Garmisch, and there were many more to follow. However, most of our subsequent trips to Garmisch were made in the fall of the year. Why we changed our European travel dates will be explained later.

For several years we made Garmisch a destination point. One can walk from one end of Garmisch village to the other without too much effort. Once we spotted a cafe that displayed delicious-looking pastries in the window. As it was an unseasonably warm day, we decided to have our coffee and pastry on the patio. Shortly after serving, we became the target of an ambush of resident bees, which were attracted to the sweets. As the local folks didn't seem too excited, we decided to try to remain calm in the midst of the invassion.

There is a marvelous little bed linen shop in Garmisch. We bought our down comforter there, which was a minor miracle in that the hours and days the shop was open was a complete mystery—absolutely no consistency for hours of business. The shop was owned and run by two mature sisters who said they could stuff our king-size comforter of choice into a twelve-by-twelve-inch box to carry on the airplane. No way did they want to ship the package.

While writing this book, I have become a thesaurus junkie. Knowing this, I still could find no other exact substitute for the word "miracle," so I find it necessary to use it again. And so, miracle of miracles, the comforter was compressed into the box just as the sisters promised. I lived in fear that an airport customs officer would want to inspect said box that, when opened, would explode like an automobile airbag on a full-size Hummer.

I have since learned that Germans are very adept at this compression technique. If you ever drive the roads in Germany, take notice of the mastery of personal packing/stowing observed through the auto windows. It appears that the local folks are very frugal and do not spend their euros on such luxury items as LUGGAGE of any sorts. They seem to gather their belongings, COMPRESS them as tightly as possible by hand, and then *cram* them into the back or bed of the car. Dad and I refer to this as the *German art of good packing.*

One evening we learned there was to be an oompah band concert in the local park. We thought it might be fun to attend, and it truly was. Upon arrival, we found a stage with about ten musicians dressed in authentic Bavarian lederhosen and hats with feathers. The usual oompah band consists of a tuba, clarinet, accordion, and trombone. The tuba sets the beat/rhythm for the music. There is always a band leader, and it is often the accordion player. The leader that evening seemed to wing it. The band would play one song and then retire to discuss what they might play next. Play, retire, sip, play, retire, sip. It was similar to a *bierhaus*. However, the only *bier* (beer) present was in the possession of the band. Toward the end of the concert, the emphasis was mostly *SIP* to *GULP.* But the music and staging was worth the lack of professionalism.

Of our many trips to Garmisch, there is one visit we make each time. This is to a small restaurant that caters mostly to locals. Don't forget about Dad's *F*s. There you will find delicious soups, Hungarian goulash, potato pancakes, and the most delicious ground beef steak. Dad and I have tried, many times, to recreate the beef steak dish but cannot even come close. I do believe this is one reason we continue to visit Garmisch every time we are in the area.

A short distance from Garmisch, in the area of Grainau, one will find the tallest point in Germany—the Zugspitz Mountain. The 9,700-foot summit can be reached either from Austria or Germany. One can actually straddle the border of the two countries while enjoying the breathtaking view from the top. Dad and I took a cable car from the Eibsee station for our adventure up the mountain. As Dad has an engineering, as well as physics and law background, he was completely mesmerized by the construction of the lift. And truly, I don't know how it was built either. We shared our cable car ride with a few other people and a dog. I wonder if I got my love of dogs from my German heritage. Dad says NO. This book is not a travel guide, but I would have been remiss if I had not mentioned the Zugspitz experience.

Garmisch remains one of our favorite trips. We have been there many times and will continue to visit when we are in Germany.

Silvesters Are Not for Sissies

Freiburg

Leaving Baden-Baden one cold day, Dad and I began to make our way to Freiburg. And you ask why we are leaving the beautiful town of Baden-Baden located deep in the magnificent black forest? And I would respond that Dad and I could not find car parking near a hotel where we might stay the night. And how is this so? There are many signs in Baden-Baden that direct one to proper parking places and hotels, but no matter how one approaches the problem and follows directions, one always ends up in a public parking garage far away from the main town area. After making three or four attempts to stash our trusty rental car of mysterious origin, we gave up and proceeded on our way to Freiburg. This was no great loss for Dad, as Freiburg is one of his favorite places and not nearly as expensive as Baden-Baden—even though Dad had generously bought a watch for me at the casino for my birthday. I had visited Baden-Baden once before with my traveling friend, Ida Jo, but Freiburg was a new experience for me.

Having spent a significant amount of time on our parking trauma, we were hasty to make our way to Freiburg before dark. Speeding down the road, no autobahn here, we find Dad at the wheel and me with the map. As I have mentioned before, MAP READING IS NOT MY THING—and especially in the evening dusk. Also, it is not helpful that road signs use German words, containing no less than fifty letters in each word and do not correspond or appear anywhere on the map. My German heritage did not gift me with

German map-reading skills—or any other map-reading skills, I might add.

A bit down the road I spied a sign that assuredly was a necessary right turn to Freiburg. At least it looked so on THE MAP. Keep in mind it now was approaching full-blown darkness. After several miles, Dad and I were thrilled to see a road sign and hoped it would confirm we were well on our way to our preferred destination. Are you ready for this? The sign clearly read Devil's Highway and in smaller letters something about *Faust.* Never before in the history of man has there ever been a U-turn of such meteoritic speed than Dad performed that night. With hair standing out on the back of Dad's neck, we streaked our way back to the main road—lost but safe. To this day, Dad's neck reacts the same way when remembering that adventure.

Needing a place to regroup, we spied a small pizza café on the road in the middle of nowhere—can you believe it? Dragging our frayed bodies inside, along with the useless map, we planned our assault on Freiburg. Following an attack of hysterical laughter, which I am prone to do when physically exhausted, hungry, and lost, we were ready to try again. I must say an old woman who was eating pizza, plus the café cook, both looked at me as if I had completely lost it. And they were pretty much on target. They were both smiling when we left the café. Perhaps they were hoping I was not entering a period of violence. No words were exchanged between the four of us, as there was that language thing problem lingering in the room.

Once more *on the road again,* as Willie Nelson might sing, we were off to Freiburg. With Dad at the reins, and on a more substantial road I might add, and my riding shotgun and clutching the infamous and useless map, we sped in hot pursuit of the elusive Freiburg. It did absolutely no good to try to read the fifty-plus-letter road signs, as they went by in a blur due to our speed-of-light pace. Also, what I thought I saw on the signs had no relationship to any words on the map. Maybe this is where the saying "*flying by the seat of your pants*" originated. But *zoom* we did—right to a sign that, in all its glory, read FREIBURG. Making a sharp left turn, we had Freiburg in our sights—at last.

As Dad had visited Freiburg many times before, he had a particular hotel in mind. In the deep dark of the night, on unfamiliar streets, we found ourselves driving down the middle of a *PEDESTRIAN-ONLY* walkway. I shudder to this day when I think about the possibility of our being caught by the police for our pedestrian-only driving performance.

The Post Hotel is little and old. I sometimes think that is why Dad married me, because I am little and old. (My friend Caroline said she was surprised Dad didn't marry her because she is "littler and older" than me.) The hotel elevator accommodates three people without luggage or two people with luggage. The bedroom and bath are quite adequate and little and old. There is a view of a little and old vineyard from the bedroom window.

The hotel is a few short blocks from the old town area. There, one will find restaurants, an ancient cathedral, and a daily outdoor market. Small canals wander through the town and offer play for children and photo ops for tourists. Dad thought the canals were built in Roman times as sewage canals. Wrong. They were actually built for safety in case of fire(s).

It is now coming together for me. Do you remember the four *F*s in Dad's life? One is food. And at the outdoor market you could taste the most divine German sausage sandwich. I understand Dad's fixation with the Post Hotel in that it is easy walking distance to the market and his beloved sausage. We have partaken of this sausage in the winter with snow on the ground and in the fall with leaves turning brilliant red and gold. And it always tastes the same—GUTE (good).

One particular restaurant experience stands out in my memory. As it was a rather cold evening, I thought a hot bowl of soup and crusty bread would be the perfect meal to warm us. Also, don't forget the wonderful (Kool-Aid?) Trollinger wine. I asked the waitress what kind of *suppen* (soup) was on the menu. She of no English and I of no German began our debate over the *suppen* choices. Finally, I pointed to a word on the menu and asked what it meant. Her answer was a rather terse "IT'S GOOT" (*GUTE*, GOOD). With that I abandoned my challenge, gave an affirmative head nod, and ordered the soup. And the waitress was right it was GUTE.

Of particular interest, located on the main square (Münsterplatz), is the catherdral (Münster). Lacy spires rise out to mark the impressive main church. Semipermanent scaffolding is a feature that adorns the pink-colored sandstone of the exterior. Keeping the fragile sandstone from falling apart is a never-ending task. The frilly tower (Münsterturm) is as tall as the church is long—127 yards. Up in the tower you will find sixteen different bells, each having a different name and purpose. For example, in November and December, the tax bell rings twice weekly to remind that taxes are due. Also traditionally, Catholics do not eat meat on Fridays, so they would eat *spaetzle*—German noodles—instead. This bell was named the spaetzle bell. And so on. The stained-glass windows are original from the thirteenth and fourteenth centuries. These windows were hidden away for their protection during World War II.

Along the back wall of the church, you will find photographs of the demolition of Freiburg after the World War II bombing. The city was spared through most of the war until November 27, 1944, when in the time of twenty minutes, approximately 80 percent of Freiburg's buildings were destroyed. Some believe a miracle of divine intervention occurred when sparing the cathedral from destruction. Others choose to believe that the bombers purposefully avoided the church.

One New Year's Eve, Dad and I found ourselves in Freiburg again with no hotel reservations—as usual. The clerk at the little and old Hotel Post was challenged to find us a room elsewhere, as the Post was holiday full. And luckily she did at the Wolf Hotel—not to be confused with the Wolf (Duck) Hotel in Oberammergau.

If you do not know what a New Year's Eve Silvester celebration is, let me enlighten you. I have never attended one of these, but Dad has verbally shared his Silvester experiences with me many times. The guests are seated, shoulder to shoulder, at *VERY LONG* tables. There are many food courses that are preceded with various classes of alcoholic beverages and followed by cigar smoke of volcanic proportions. Talking LOUD, singing **LOUDER**, and HEADACHES scoring a twenty on a scale of one to ten proclaimed no Silvesters for me.

With Dad sporting a man-size head cold, we walked to the Münsterplatz to find a restaurant where we could carry out some cheese, cold cuts, bread, and wine. With no more Silvesters in our future, we decided we would spend the evening in the quiet of our room. Spotting a restaurant close by, we asked if we could have our fare to go. With a rather stern and pompous gesture, the answer was a resounding German NO! With my German heritage tenacity, I asked if we could have the food served at the table—answer, "of course." After serving, we asked if we could have a paper bag and a box—answer, "of course." So we packed our food and wine, paid our bill, and went on our way to the Wolf Hotel for our New Year's Eve in-room festivities.

Dad, of the head cold, decided that sleep was the cure he needed. So I, alone, sat in my bed eating bread and cheese and washed down the German wine—Trollinger, of course. This wine, of questionable vintage, was similar to strawberry Kool-Aid in color and taste. With Dad asleep, I found no reason to stay awake until midnight. So warmed by the wine and filled with the cheese and bread, I drifted off to sleep through the changing of the New Year—or so I thought.

At the stroke of midnight, the attack of World War III exploded. There were cannons, rockets, and nonstop firecrackers that would challenge any military war assault. The noise and flashing lights encompassed the entire city of Freiburg. I might also add that it continued for several LONG hours. Shortly before dawn, apparently the fireworks stash was depleted. Dad, of the head cold, and I staggered to our beds for a bit of sleep. And a bit it was

As this hotel had also hosted a Silvester, there was major cleanup of landmine proportions on the horizon. After about two hours of sleep, we were awakened by high-heeled shoes clopping on marble floors directly above our room. This constant noise continued until we finally gave up and checked out.

We decided to make one last visit to the cathedral on the Münsterplatz to be sure it was still standing after the explosion of the New Year's festivities. We stepped from our car onto a carpet, approximately four inches deep, of spent firecracker wrapping. The entire Platz was covered in the wrappers. No wonder we thought it was the beginning of World War III.

A few years later, we changed our winter European trip to the fall season. As usual, we went to the little, old Hotel Post, only to have great difficulty in recognizing it. It so seems that the entire city of Freiburg had changed its looks from a charming Christmas village to a riotous college town, overrun with students on bicycles who are rather intent on running you over. In order to avoid being assaulted by a roving herd of *masochistic* student bicyclers, we decided to make our way down the road to find, perhaps, another little and old hotel for the night—and as usual, we did.

Potato Pancakes, Where Are You?

Munich-Munchen

The flight plan of my first European trip with Dad took us to Frankfurt, Germany. This was the *romantik* road loop, sending us to Rothenburg ob der Tauber, mentioned previously. Ending our two-week tour on the *romantik* road, we spent the night at a rather respectable hotel located on the Frankfurt airport property. The noteworthy hotel provided its guests with pale mustard-colored water in the bathtub and shower. This issue caused Dad to grumble at me for not cleaning the tub after my shower, where, in fact, there was permanent tub discoloration due to the frequent pale-mustard bath. Grumble not deserved.

Next morning at the airport we found long lines of derelict-looking people, floor-bound from lack of sleep. And my vision of Frankfurt-bound airplanes being demolished by onboard bombs did not lend to my peace of mind. All of this prompted me to look for a better way for us to get to Germany. And so it happened. We found Munich in our headlights.

Munich has become our favorite big city in all of Europe. The airport is clean and extremely organized. The airline clubs are comfortable, and the food and beverages served there can be a full meal anytime of the day or night. One slight drawback is that the rental car agency is a LONG walk from the baggage concourse. After flying twelve or thirteen hours, the long walk can prove to be quite a challenge. And I'm usually in "stagger mode" upon plane arrival, whereas Dad seems to fare better and looks after me when I begin to drift and wander off.

Hotels in Germany, for the most part, are wonderful—Frankfurt airport hotel excepted. Cleanliness is a given, and the difference between two stars and five stars lay in the furnishing, amenities, and service. We have gone from five stars to three in one day and with equal comfort.

Hotel Bayerischerhoff is a cavernous hotel, in the Bavarian style, and houses a delightful stube where one can dine on small Nürnberg sausages, perfect sauerkraut, and roasted potatoes. Dad has a client, whom I lovingly refer to as Big M, who often meets with us in Munich for business. Big M prefers the Bayerischerhoff. The hotel is located across the street from the Loden Frey store, where the Minnesota-based client's wife buys clothes. Said client suggested I shop there while the men attended to their business. Acting on his suggestion, I visited Loden Frey only to discover very expensive clothing that was suitable for the cold of Munich, Minnesota, or even bitter Antarctica but certainly not Southern California.

One evening while staying at a different hotel, we decided to taxi in for dinner at the Bayerischerhoff stube. Approximately two or three blocks from the hotel, the traffic was completely stopped. The driver asked that we walk the rest of the way, and we did. There we found a massive crowd surrounding the hotel waiting for a glimpse of Russian president Putin, who was about to exit. We did have a Putin sighting, but it was not worth the sacrifice of a stube dinner.

My most favorite hotel in the world is and was the Rafael in Munich. It is right up there with the Brenner's Park Hotel in Baden-Baden. The Rafael is located on a street that is almost impossible to find. Once found, it is easy walking distance to the town *Marienplatz*, the *Hafbrauhaus* (beer garden), and the *Haxnbauer* restaurant, a favorite of Dad's. It also is within easy walking distance to the German version of *Rodeo Drive* shopping where Dad insists I'll get lost so should not wander there. I believe he is only thinking of my possible purchases that might put a heavy *dent* in our credit card.

The Rafael has fifty-three luxurious rooms, impeccable service, and a cocktail lounge complete with subdued piano music. The reception staff appear to know you upon arrival. You do not have to sign for your beverage fare as you are a known guest and the amount, charged correctly, appears on your checkout statement. Shoes are left outside your door at night to be cleaned and polished by the shoe elf, I presume. At first, Dad was a tad apprehensive about leaving his shoes outside our room overnight. But they were there waiting for him each morning along with an English newspaper.

One of my Rafael flashbacks has to do with one of Dad's foreign associates. Ulrich was an associate based in Pfortzheim. When Dad and Ulrich had business to conduct, Ulrich preferred to come to Munich, as he truly enjoyed our treat of fine cuisine at the Rafael. Ulrich always appeared in his proper tweed jacket, handmade shoes, and fashion-of-the-day shirt and tie.

However, on one visit we had trouble locating Ulrich in the lobby. Then lo and behold, we spied the new Ulrich in all his glory. Ulrich appeared in a leather bomber jacket, skinny pants that would rival Michael Flatley's *Riverdance* costume, jodhpurs, and no tie. In addition, Ulrich, who usually traveled by train, explained he had driven to Munich with his *GIRLFRIEND*, who was looking for a parking place as we spoke. Shortly, *GIRLFRIEND* appeared and pleasantries were exchanged. It was at that very moment I realized *GIRLFRIEND* did not speak English—not one word.

Dad and Ulrich decided they would go to our room to further their business meeting, and it was suggested GF a.k.a. GIRLFRIEND and I should visit in the hotel lobby. In what language I might ask? As I previously had taken several French lessons from Mme. Dr. Hart (where I was at best a C student) and GF knew perhaps twelve words in French, we agreed this was to be our language of social communication. I could not sell her on Spanish, which is a language requirement for all California residents, or at least it should be.

At this point, I should advise you of my French skills. I attempted using these newly acquired skills once in Carcassonne, France, when ordering from a menu. I must tell you it nearly started a riot. The waiter ***PRETENDED*** not to understand me, and the patrons offered their dubious help. In exasperation, I finally pointed to a customer's plate and explained I'll have that. By the way, *with Spanish being my second language and spoken with a rather pronounced Texas accent, my* French lessons were a miserable failure—as you may have guessed.

So now with my new charge, GF, we set out on our visitation ritual using a combined language gift of roughly twenty-five words and no complete sentences. After nearly two hours, Dad and Ulrich returned, which was indeed very timely, as GF and I had used our twenty-five words so many times that we had completely exhausted our supply of subject matter.

Some years ago, the hotel Rafael was purchased by the Oriental Mandarin Hotel Corporation and the prices zoomed out of reason—at least our reason. We thought we only wanted to rent a lovely room, not purchase a hotel.

An alternate base hotel for us in Munich might be the Excelsior Hotel, which was recommended to us. Upon check-in, the bellman was most proud and emphatic about the new Pizza Hut across the street. We soon found out the hotel had no dining room (except for breakfast) and the Pizza Hut was the only restaurant in walking distance. The staff also explained to us that the Marienplatz, home to all Munich activity, was about a ten-minute walk. Yes, siree, you can walk it in ten minutes if you are an Olympic gold medal winner in track events. Obviously, this hotel was a one-time stay. And by the way, we were grateful for the Pizza Hut.

After the Excelsior Hotel, we tried a Marriott hotel a ways from the town center but very acceptable—and with good down pillows too. Almost the best part was George the bellman. George, a black gentleman, was from Houston, which gave me a connection immediately. George has been good to us for many years. He still goes home to Houston for Thanksgiving to see his mother and eat his "mama's good cooking."

Restaurants in Munich usually have delicious cuisine. Often there are English menus available—if not, good luck. Wiener schnitzel and sausage and sauerkraut are usually easy to translate. Water with ice is a bit more of a challenge. Also you might want "still water," as other waters are much like drinking club soda, with the same aftereffect.

Once while walking toward the Marienplatz, we spied a small restaurant named the Wine Stube. Through the window, we saw white linen tablecloths with flowers and candles. Soft German melodies drifted through the door. Our kind of place, we agreed. It was and still is. One evening there, we ordered an interesting appetizer served in a small ceramic pot along with a basket of warm French baguettes. Now let me tell you, warm bread of any kind is a go, no matter where I am dining. We began with a smear of unknown pot content on warm French bread. Even after a somewhat familiar bacon flavor, we had no idea what we were devouring with such gusto. Upon finishing this creamy feast, I announced that the taste reminded me of bacon grease one might have saved after frying the morning bacon. And that, my friends, is just what it was! I have since learned that this is almost a German staple.

The Hauxenbauer is another good restaurant in Munich where pork knuckles are roasted on a spit for at least three hours. The pork drippings fall below onto sauerkraut, which becomes smoky pork flavored. At one time in his life, Dad was able to eat an entire pork knuckle, which is quite a feat. However, we now order one half knuckle, which is ample for the two us in our semisedentary years. Dad's gold standard of German cuisine is roasted potatoes, which are grilled with bits of onion and ham. The potatoes at the Hauxenbauer are number two on his potato list.

As I have previously mentioned the stube at the Bayerischerhoff Hotel, I should like to add that their own in-house bakery produces a variety of baked breads along with my gold-standard pretzel. Dad's number one gold standard, roasted potatoes, is also found at the stube.

The Rathskeller located on the Marienplatz has saved our lives on several cold occasions. Memorably one day after Christmas, when much of Munich was closed for the holidays, the Rathskeller provided warmth and good food on a FRIGID-to-the-bone night. Actually when rounding a corner on foot, I think the bitter cold "froze" my sinuses—or almost.

I should also like to mention something to you about the sturdy German folks. Apparently their being outside is an obsession. In the cold of winter, I have seen outdoor tables with chairs covered in faux fur and blankets under which to snuggle. I have trouble figuring out how they enjoy cold food that was born to be hot. I guess with enough beer it really doesn't matter—cold food or cold bodies. Don't forget, I am a Southern California girl who was born and raised in the heat of Texas.

Big M, Dad's Minnesota client, told us about a wonderful restaurant that served the most delicious potato pancakes and was located next to **THE** big church. Firstly, there are at least four big churches surrounding the Marienplatz. So carefully, one by one, on the cold and snow-covered ground, we searched for said restaurant. Nowhere could we find a restaurant serving potato pancakes—and we gave up. Several years later, Big M joined us in Munich, and we challenged him to steer us to the elusive café. We surely did locate the restaurant, but it did not and never did ever serve potato pancakes—OOPS!

Speaking of the surrounding churches, they are large, opulent, and very old. Some were seriously damaged or destroyed during World War II. The oldest church is the Frauenkirsch. The official name is Cathedral of Our Lady, and it was built in 1468. Once, I went to for Frauenkirsch to light a candle for a Catholic friend who was embarking on an African mission to help the children and the aged. The candle was lit with trepidation, as I am not Catholic with a *C* but a kindred Christian and catholic with a little *c*. I told Dad I hoped the church ghosts would not be mad at me and burn down the church. Next day, I found it all to be okay.

The Marienplatz is a wonderful gathering place. The surrounding stores consist of souvenir shops, department stores, fine bed linen stores, and Woolworth's, where I purchased my favorite everyday wineglasses (Roemer glasses) and nail glue for emergencies. The glockenspiel in the Rathaus tower performs regularly with dancing folks and jousting horses. This lends a colorful sight, no matter how many times one sees it. The Marienplatz also serves as a stage for demonstrations of various causes. One recent Saturday in the fall, the demonstrators, ringed by police, were loudly protesting an increase in bank fees and charges. Sound familiar?

An easy walk from the Marienplatz will bring you to a Hofbrauhaus (beer garden). I've been told the food there is quite good, but we go mostly for an occasional beer, the jolly atmosphere, and the oompah band, which from time to time plays "The Eyes of Texas."

One of my favorite, if not my all-time favorite, is the outdoor market. Unlike the Italian markets where one can buy sturdy undergarments, a selection of food and wine poured from a jug in the back of a pickup truck. The German outdoor markets have cheeses, fish, fresh meats, fruits, vegetables, brilliant flowers, and delicious wurst sandwiches grilled while you wait. It is impossible for us to walk by this delicious aroma and not stop for a sandwich.

Photography is one of my loves, and the German market is one of my favorite places for photos. I must have taken a zillion photographs—crowd shots, store shots, close-up shots, etc. One particular photo subject was of a bearded man dressed in authentic lederhosen and which, I'm certain, had never been cleaned—maybe the man too. This man had the most perfect face for a photo. I asked if I could take his picture, and his response was a head bob and a request for five marks—no euros, then. As a twenty mark was all I had, I gave it to him. He pocketed it and began to pose. With my arms waving and flapping, I managed to retrieve my fifteen marks change. This photograph is still, to this day, one of my favorites and hangs proudly in our home.

There is an acute problem, which, in my opinion, has become critical mass and in my vocabulary is called CHICKEN. I have always praised autobahn drivers as they blazed down the road with never or rare accidents. However, this chicken game, which is confined to villages and cities, is of major concern.

Being a Southern California girl, I understand that pedestrians have the right to cross the streets without being made a unique form of roadkill. Not so in Germany, where drivers are aggressive toward anyone on foot (and not necessarily other drivers). Now if the cars or taxis don't get you, the bicycles will. Rules for pedestrians are, number one, never make eye contact with the car driver; keep your head down and walk and pray—actually use most of your energy for praying. Rule number two, never walk in a dedicated bicycle lane—most especially in a city. If you do, while I can almost guarantee that you won't be killed, you will probably be struck down and certainly left with a permanent disability.

Bicyclists in Munich take no prisoners. And thirdly, wear practical walking shoes, as many of the streets and walkways are paved with cobblestones. As a basic minimum, practice doing dignified pratfalls, as I can almost guarantee you will need this skill.

And one last word, if you do drive in Germany, bring your own GPS system, as all auto manuals are written in German. The same is true of the GPS found in rental cars.

An Alien Monster in My Bed

Oberammergau

At the risk of being called a trollop, I find myself confessing yet to another love affair. The lover's name is Oberammergau. The affair began many years ago and is shared with Dad. Could this be a menage a trois?

Late one evening while driving from Tyrol, we began looking for a place to put our heads for the night. Again, no hotel reservations. Hotels, Gastehauses, and such are listed on small street signs in German villages. As Dad was accustomed to searching out rooms for the night, he was quite familiar with the signs. Actually, he is a bird dog when it comes to restaurants and hotels. He can sniff out a restaurant that he may have visited twenty years previously, while I have trouble locating my car in a parking garage.

Spotting a sign listing Hotel Antonia Garni, we took a quick right turn down a narrow dark street. And as the sign promised, a little yellow hotel was waiting for us. Erika, owner and innkeeper, allowed that there was a room available on the first floor. The room met all the requirements I had established some years prior to our first trip to Europe. Yes, sir, there was the soft down comforter, the fluffy down pillows, and, most important of all, a bathroom with shower. Plus, everything was squeaky clean. We were thrilled.

Having driven most of the day, we were anxious for sleep. As Dad and I are fresh air people, opening the door to the patio seemed the logical thing to do—no matter how cold it was. Snuggling under the warm comforter, sleep came quickly. Sometime later, I was awakened by a *giant alien monster*, with a body of fur and claws like eagle talons—or so I imagined—walking on my bed. Shrieking for Dad to wake up, he bounced out of bed, stumbling his way to find a light.

The *giant alien monster* turned out to be a rather large tabby cat that had come in for a visit. It was a good thing the cat had a docile disposition, as Dad gathered him up and began to stuff him out the door—with some resistance, I might add, from the cat. Once again, we began our go-to-sleep ritual with the door slightly more closed. Sure enough, sometime later, *giant alien monster* squeezed his way through the door, hopped on the bed, and curled up next to me for the night. As I am an animal lover, I welcomed the cat, as I figured he was cold and needed a warm place to spend the night.

Next morning, we were awakened by the delicious smell of coffee brewing. Remembering that *garni* means the hotel will serve breakfast, we were quick to dress and find the origin of the aroma. With visions of Juan Valdez, the Folger coffee man, wandering through the coffee fields of Colombia, we found a tiny breakfast room with buffet fare and warmed by a lovely blue-and-white antique ceramic stove. Breakfast buffets in Germany are not in the least related to the lavish buffets in the United States that are usually found for Sunday brunches. Erika's breakfast consisted of rustic bread, cold cuts and cheese sliced so thinly they might be mistaken for tissue paper, a bit of canned fruit, an occasional tomato, tea, and STRONG COFFEE. We soon learned that if we didn't arrive early, the food became very meager, and it was not replenished.

On each table perched a ceramic pot in which trash—teabags, sugar wrappers, etc.—was to be deposited. This pot is found on almost every breakfast table in Germany. And if the guest does not properly use the trash pot, he or she is the receiver of many scowls and presumably terse words—in German, of course. After a few angry glares from Erika, who loomed over the guests, we learned and remembered to use the pots. By the way, try not to drip coffee or jelly on the tablecloth! As Dad is a world-class food dripper, this became a very challenging chore.

After many years of regular visits to Oberammergau and Hotel Antonio Garni, Erika became very friendly and offered an egg to Dad from time to time. The egg was boiled and never the same—hard-boiled, soft, or somewhere in between. Dad would ask what kind of egg he would get, and Erika always answered, "I don't know, we'll see in a minute." Dad was always grateful for the kindness and the egg. Also, **DO NOT DROP EGGSHELLS ON THE TABLECLOTH**. Don't forget the aforementioned trash pot.

However, it is quite remarkable that Erika can grow orchids, which bloom, in the dry and cold climate of Oberammergau; and yet I have such difficulties doing so in beautiful sunny Southern California. Erika's orchids bring smiles of cheer to her many breakfast guests.

Following several trips to Oberammergau, Erica upgraded us to the "big apartment." This apartment has a bed area; a sitting area for our gin rummy games; and a kitchen nook where we enjoyed hot chocolate, tea, wine and bits of cheese. And, of course, the obligatory bathroom with shower. All in all, quite delightful. The downside to this luxury apartment is that it is necessary to drag luggage up three flights of stairs. In addition, the bed area is somewhat of a *minefield*. The ceiling is slanted so that when getting out of bed, you have to walk bent over for a few steps. If you stood up too quickly, you would bang your head mightily. Also, for guests of the male gender, *self-neutering* might occur if they were not extremely careful when exiting the wooden-sided bed. After a few trips to the hotel, we managed to master the trash pot, the slanted ceilings and the "nutcracker" on the bedside.

Oberammergau itself is a charming village. Early morning walks are pleasant, with views of Brown Swiss cows grazing in the pastures, families working in their gardens, and folks riding their bicycles to work. The good news is that, in Germany, all the cows have their own bells, where in other countries only the lead cow has one. Therein lies the cliché "the bell cow," which is sometimes used as a description of a leader. Or as they say, *if you are not the bell cow, the view is always the same.*

The half-timbered Luftmalrei village houses are frescoed with biblical scenes and fairy-tale characters and are found throughout the village. Those became popular in the eighteenth century. There are two main sites that are truly worth the time to see. First is the town church. Being that Oberammergau is a major wood-carving center, all the church statues are made of wood and then stuccoed and gilded to look like marble or gold.

The second is the Passion Platz where the Passion play is performed every ten years, starting in May, for one hundred days. Only people born in Oberammergau are eligible to perform in the play, which depicts the story of Jesus's entry into Jerusalem, crucifixion, and resurrection. The exception is if one has been a resident for at least twenty years and was born in Germany; in this instance they might be considered for a "crowd" part. A cast of two thousand is involved in the production of this extravagant five-hour Passion play, and the daily attendance is five thousand. This in and of itself is somewhat of a miracle, as there are only 1,200 beds in Oberammergau.

Dad and I were blessed one day to join an English-speaking tour of the Passion Platz that included the seating areas (which are covered), the stage (which is not covered), and backstage. Backstage we were privileged to visit the costume room and the prop room, which housed the Crucifixion cross sharing its secrets of how the actor, portraying Jesus, was able to be nailed and suspended for a lengthy period of time on stage. All in all, this was a travel highlight that is near the top of my travel highlights list.

I mention wood carvings, and yes, there are wood carvings aplenty. Almost every other shop either displays carvings in their window or has the actual wood-carver working for all to see. Many, if not most of the whittled works, are of a religious nature. While walking one day, I found a wonderful wood-carver working in his window. It is a family enterprise. He carves the characters and his wife does the painting. His son will be a carver someday but for now is a carpenter. I'm told this is the first step to learning the carving business. Adding year to year, I have purchased a nativity tableau, complete with donkey and angel, from this pleasant wood-carver. I don't care if Pope Benedict says there were no animals in the stable at the Christmas birth; I still believe there was at least a *DONKEY.*

Dining in Oberammergau is a bit challenging. Our first venture into dining was at the Wolf Hotel. Many times we walked by this hotel with its glorious flower boxes filled with brilliant red geraniums. Conveniently located in regard to our Hotel Antonio, we felt we might give it a try. The meal was quite good, and we felt it deserved a return visit. The following morning we shared with Erika our pleasant dining experience. With a frown on her face, she allowed that she did not like the *Duck Hotel.* We explained to her that we had eaten at the Wolf Hotel and not the Duck Hotel. This is when we learned to listen more carefully to people who speak a bit of English but with a heavy accent. The infamous Duck Hotel is actually a hotel that accepts DOGS, and Erika's pronouncement of "dog" sounded like "duck." In addition, the hotel sponsors weekly dog-training sessions where the dogs and their owners are hotel guests. Erika's theory is that if you allow dogs in your hotel they eventually end up in the bed, and she will have no part of that.

Erika, the innkeeper, then gave us directions to a lovely restaurant down a ways in the main part of town. The restaurant was charming, and the food was superb. Interestingly, we tried later to dine there on several occasions and were successful less than 50 percent of the time. There seemed to be no rhyme or reason as to when and if the restaurant was open. So back to the Duck Hotel.

Again, at breakfast, Erika gave us directions to a *secret* restaurant that was held close to the bosom of the local folks. No tourists there, please. Well, Dad and I walked many, many miles (maybe 250 miles in the dark) in hot pursuit of this well-hidden restaurant. As it turned out, we hiked more miles than necessary, as we had personal navigation difficulties, plus an inability to comprehend German street signs. Having said that, we found the *secret* eating house, and miracle of all, it was open. After seating, we discovered that absolutely no one spoke English—waiters, host, or guests. Stumbling our way through the German menu, we somehow managed to order a scrumptious meal. Lucky we were when ordering, as there was no familiar Wiener schnitzel to be found. Also, the wine list did not sport my favorite grocery market Trollinger. It appeared this was a rather tony restaurant. Once again at breakfast, we told Erika of our excellent dining experience. She was thrilled, and we said we looked forward to an encore—especially since we had now perfected the walking directions. We are still looking forward to a repeat meal, as the restaurant has never been open when we tried to go back. So back again to the Duck Hotel.

The Wolf (Duck) Hotel has served us well for many years. We have learned to enjoy the several dogs that are stationed under the dining tables. Also, there are two beautiful German shepherds that seem to manage the reservation desk. They are well mannered and rarely give a WOOF. I might add that our dog, Ruffles, has been trained to go to restaurants in San Diego. She also curls up under the table and never presents a problem. But SHE NEVER GETS IN OUR BED.

A mysterious oddity occurred one day while taking an afternoon stroll through the village. On a corner, a quaint café that serves coffee, tea, pastries, and ice cream was located. While ordering our coffee, we spied a pan of the most delicious-looking tiramisu—probably assembled in mama's kitchen with loving hands. Ignoring the gigantic calorie intake, Dad and old muffin top here decided we were required to share said delicacy. If there is a heaven on earth, we experienced it. Each bite of the tiramisu was angelic to our senses.

The following year, we anxiously sped our way to the corner café for coffee and the celestial tiramisu. Upon arrival, we noted there was none in the pastry window. In panic, we asked the server if the desert was finished and would there be more the next day. The gentleman responded as if there had *NEVER* been tiramisu in the café and probably never would be. Heartbroken and crushed, we once again *slothed* our way back to the secure arms of the Duck Hotel.

Several day trips from Oberammergau stand out in my mind. One is a visit to Wieskirche. This is Germany's greatest rococo-style church and has been newly restored. While it is a bit overripe with decoration, it is bursting with beauty. The church was built around the statue of scourged Christ, which supposedly wept in 1738. Pilgrims came from all around to witness the statue miraculously shed tears.

The second is a tour of Linderhof Castle. As Dad had traveled Europe more than me, I was somewhat tuned to believe him when he said that the signs pointing to *SCHLOSS LINDERHOF* had nothing to do with a castle, even though Schloss translates to "castle." As I mentioned a bit earlier, it is an accident of birth that I am not royalty. Therefore, I can sniff out a castle much the way Dad can sniff out a restaurant. One driving day, Dad gave in to motoring the Schloss Linderhof road. Lo and behold, there it was in all its glory, a beautiful white palace surrounded by fountains and Italian-sculptured gardens. The castle was built by King Ludwig, or "crazy King Ludwig" as my earlier traveling companion, Ida Jo, called him

A tour through the castle is a treat for the eyes. Linderhof is rather small as castles go but exquisite in every way. King Ludwig lived to be only forty years old and was deemed to be *mad* by his countrymen. The story goes that he accidentally drowned (or was possibly murdered) for spending most of Germany's money building his many castles—one of which is the model for the Disneyland castle.

Ida Jo and I agreed King Ludwig was not mad; he just knew how to live well. We decided we could sit on his throne and eat chicken and chocolate cake—which was our meal of choice—any time we wanted. You see, we rationalized that if you ate enough roasted chicken, you have calories left over for the chocolate cake.

One day a driving trip found us in a small village surrounded by a large and beautiful lake. On the lake there were two—maybe three—fishermen in rowboats. We were excited to find this and explore the possibility of Dad enjoying a day of fishing—one of his four *F*s. At breakfast, we told Erika of our find. Slowly, she shook her head, proclaiming that in order for one to go fishing in Germany, they had to go to *FISHING SCHOOL*, and the license process took SIX years. Obviously, fishing is not encouraged in Germany.

I would be remiss if I didn't give you a glimpse into the wonderful world of computers and Wi-Fi in Oberammergau. Erika's computer gives new meaning to the word "slow." This mechanical wonder resides in the party room/basement of her hotel. Most of the time it is in need of a repairman, who will stop by on rare occasions. If the e-mail addiction overcomes a guest, they can always wander down to the Post Hotel where they sell computer time in fifteen-minute increments. We found the answer to computer mania by bringing our BlackBerry, which works well in

Europe. In fact, we received pictures of our pup, Ruffles, the day she was born on our trusty "Berry."

Speaking of electronics, it was in Oberammergau where I mastered my first encounter with a GPS device—and in German too, therefore crowning me with the title of "electronic genius." Now we bring our own GPS, which does the job for us in Europe. Prior to this magical device, we spent most of our time lost.

Oberammergau has been a welcoming haven for us for many years. We love the morning walks, the restaurant challenges, the nocturnal visiting cat, and especially our good friend Erika. We look forward to these warm fuzzies again.

His Loafers Were a Little Light

Heidleburg

This is a little story I considered writing into a group of stories that addressed various destinations with only a short bit of time spent in each one. However, after beginning, I realized this story deserved its own chapter.

After a long day of driving, Dad and I began to look for a place to put our heads for the night. This was during the time of driving and searching with no reservations in place. There, in a most charming village, was an attractive bed and breakfast by the name of Heidi House. Dad sprung from the car while I exhaustedly waited.

Dad was met at the door by a gentleman who immediately thought Dad might be a *festive* roommate for an evening of *light-loafered frivolity.* Yes, of course, there was a room available and wouldn't Dad like to see it? The innkeeper's enthusiasm literally melted into a puddle when Dad said he would like to show the room to his wife before making a decision.

In full husband-protective mode, Dad and I entered an attractive inn that would surely fill our needs, except that we would have to share a bathroom with anyone who might rent the bedroom next door. When I exclaimed that sharing a bathroom with persons of unknown *breeding* was unacceptable, the deflated amorous innkeeper announced he would not rent the other available bedroom to anyone, thus allowing us a bathroom exclusively for ourselves. And so we stayed.

It was then that a series of small miracles began to occur. Dad and I asked if there were any shops open that sold cuckoo clocks. Our innkeeper, previously amorous, said he knew of one shop where the proprietor handmade the most wonderful clocks, and he would personally take us there. Hand in hand, the three of us shuffled through the snow and *BITTER* cold to meet the shopkeeper and his remarkable payload of amazing clocks. They were beautifully made and were a *whopping* seventy-five dollars. For some DUMB reason, Dad and I thought seventy-five dollars was way too much for the clock, so the three of us trudged back to the inn, and the clockmaker went back to his warm bed from which he had been awakened. We were seriously stupid for not buying the handsome clock.

After arriving in our warm and welcome room, there came a gentle rap on the door. Our amorous innkeeper invited us to a small sitting room where we might enjoy American music played on TV by the Hungarian Symphony Orchestra. Of course we would. Settling down in comfortable overstuffed chairs, we heard a slight tap on the door. There we again found amorous innkeeper serving a bottle of (ARE YOU READY FOR THIS?) apricot brandy. I consider this another miracle, as Apricot Brandy is my very favorite liqueur and is rarely found even in the most select cocktail lounges. Needless to say, our one-night stay at Heidi House left us with pleasant memories.

Leaving Heidi House the next morning, Sunday, we decided to explore Heidleburg further. As I have mentioned before, these Germans are sturdy folks. In well-below-freezing temperature, there were wall-to-wall people pounding the pavement in the major shopping areas, and **NOTHING WAS OPEN.** The women were beautifully dressed complete with fur coats, fashionable hats, and high-heel shoes. The men sported handsome overcoats, hats, and expensive clothing. No jeans or jogging shoes for these folks! We have witnessed this same behavior in Frankfurt, where we found a multistory mall of extreme contemporary architecture and jammed with walkers on all four floors. Again, **NOTHING WAS OPEN**. I should add that this mall was partially enclosed, so the *pavement pounders* were not completely frozen stiff in the frigid night air.

Joy to Mom's World

Christmas Markets

The year is 2009, and visions of sugar plums are beginning to dance around in my head. I have always been a Christmas person, with memories of wonderful family Christmases, complete with a visit from Santa Claus, steaming waffles swimming in butter and syrup for Christmas morning breakfast, and a beautifully clothed baby doll delivered to me by Santa himself while I fitfully slept. So it is no wonder my ears sprang to full alert when a dinner conversation with Dad's client, Big M, turned to Germany and the Christmas markets held during the Advent season prior to Christmas.

Big M shared that some years prior he had taken his wife and two sons to Munich for the Christmas market. "Christmas" and "market" are two prominent words in my vocabulary. I filed that away in my memory bank, believing that Dad would never want to go to Germany during the cold and snowy season. You see, Dad truly loves the warm to hot weather. He has said that if he had discovered Hawaii when he was about eighteen years old, he would have never gone to college or law school. He would have stayed in Hawaii and become a fishing guide. *Glad that didn't take!*

But back to 2009. For some reason, Dad and I began to talk about Germany for Christmas. As a flashback, perhaps you remember the beautiful venue we witnessed during our first visit to Rothenburg—snow falling, zither music, and a child singing "Silent Night," a virtual Christmas card. I guess that did the trick.

Travel plans and hotel reservations were in my sight. As it turned out, airplane fares were quite reasonable for that time period, and the hotel in Munich gave special Christmas market rates. Finding that our Christmas card hotel, the Markstrum in Rothenburg, had rooms available, we were on our way.

Arriving in Munich we were greeted by our old friend, bellman George, at the hotel. There is something of comfort in seeing the same friendly hotel staff year after year. As Dad had been *gifted* with a disturbing cough, we decided to wait until the next day before charging into town and the markets. Also, after a long flight, a bit of rest is always welcomed, as I do stagger and tend to bump into things following thirteen airplane hours.

Next morning we agreed that Dad (cough, cough) should stay at the hotel for rest and I should venture out on my own to explore the market. This in and of itself is rather risky, mainly due to the language barrier. However, armed with an umbrella, a long black coat with furry hood, a camera, and a taxi, I was off. The cold weather and drizzling rain did not hold me back. With the hotel and Dad in my rearview mirror and market *mania* on the horizon, I was speeding toward Christmas market *Mecca.*

I have read that Nürnberg was and still is the *MOTHER* of all Christmas markets. I find that hard to believe in that the taxi drove me into an entire Marienplatz of Christmas vendors, or one might say *Christmas market/shopper's heaven*. There were countless colorful vendor stalls each selling a variety of Christmas ornaments, Christmas music CDs, Christmas shopping bags, and a special mulled, hot sweet wine, which was drunk on the street while shopping. Now let me tell you if that wine did not put you into a happy shopping frame of mind and one cupful is all you need, then you are just an OLD SCROOGE. So shop and sip. I did.

I purchased a couple of CDs that were promised to work in the United States, a small wooden tree that twirled and played "Silent

Night" when wound, a little shopping bag to carry my *loot*, and a few small ornaments to take back home. Now it was time for my wine treat. A local shop window had the most delightful display of expensive Steiff stuffed animals, all of which were animated. Rabbits played musical instruments, bears played jumping rope games, and a variety of critters were dancing in the native Bavarian dress. Quite a large crowd gathered, and I was determined that the little "*ankle biters*" were not going to push me out or cause me to spill my wine. As I am only five foot two, I felt I had the right to the front row as well as those parka-puffed kids dripping caramel-covered apples on all who were in striking distance.

So there I was standing my ground and sipping my wine when I noticed a gray-haired gentleman giving me a big SMILE. He began to speak to me in some language of which I had never heard. He looked rather Italian but he was not speaking Italian. All the while, I kept saying, "Me ONLY ENGLISH." At any rate, he began to follow me around while I made my last attack on the vendors. It occurred to me that I could probably lose him if I *serpentined* my way through the crowd—which I did in James Bond spylike fashion. Yes, my friend, I did lose him, but don't let this cloud the experience. I HAD JUST BEEN HIT ON, and that is pretty exhilarating for a woman in her *seventies*!

So back to the hotel to check on Dad (of the cough) and to share my afternoon adventures. Dad did get better and accompanied me one night to the Christmas market so that he could see the animated animals and smell the delicious sausages cooked by the street vendors. Shopper he is NOT.

Two days before Christmas, we packed our trusty rental car (a four-door smart car that is not yet available in the United State but soon to come, I hope) and made our way to Rothenburg for the holiday. Guess what?! Rothenburg also had a Christmas market. Upon research in a travel book, Rothenburg is described as one of the best markets in all of Germany. It is a great Christmas market but is no way in the class of Munich. In fact, we learned that almost every town and village in Germany has a Christmas market. Actually, there are Rhine River cruises that one can navigate in order to visit several Christmas markets in a five-day outing. I guess I'd better not push my luck with that.

By the way, I may have mentioned earlier that Pope Benedict has said the Nativity stable housed no animals—that it is just a myth that animals were present at the birth of Christ. Well, I'm not one to argue with the pope, but as I have said I bet there was at least a *DONKEY*! And how can the pope be so sure anyway?

Once situated in our lovely Rothenburg hotel resplendent with holiday decorations, Dad and I went our separate ways so that we could buy little Christmas treasures for each other. Interesting that the Christmas vendors had mostly the same merchandise as the ones in Munich—also priced much the same. With each of us loaded with little Christmas gifts, Dad and I accidentally met on a corner where I noticed a small artificial tree branch peeking out of a shopping bag.

This tree is a story in itself. First of all, Dad was never in the class of Christmas euphoria that I am. Secondly, any little Christmas tree branch in Germany commands the price that a new Porsche (or at least a gently used one) might cost. And thirdly, Dad had bought the tree for me, knowing how much I would love it. This was far better than being hit on by a stranger of mysterious breeding. There was no question that Dad loved me more than I could ever imagine and that he had truly hit the grand slam of all times.

With a kiss for Dad, a smile on my face, and tears of happiness in my eyes, I realized that all shops would be closing in fifteen minutes and would not open again until two or more days after Christmas. We have never quite figured out Germany's closing schedule for weekends and holidays. But believe me, when stores are closed, THEY ARE CLOSED.

Shoving all the packages into Dad's arms, I declared I would return to the hotel in fifteen minutes. Off I sprinted in my best Olympic trial effort to Kathe Wohlfahrt's Christmas shop, which is known worldwide, or at least all of Europe and most of the United States (you can find it online). In less than fifteen minutes, I bought frugal—if there is such a word in Germany—ornaments for our tree. And there it was, our Christmas tree, complete with ornaments, presents, a mouse, pewter Bavarian dancers for accents, and two chocolate-covered *Schneeballen* (the braided pie crust balls previously mentioned in another chapter). Life is good.

As most of the guests had made Christmas Eve dinner reservations at the hotel and we had been told it was quite a special occasion, we decided to join in the festivities. The hotel chef and the hotel manager (husband and wife representing two genders) are also the hotel owners. And they really outdid themselves, which I understand is their tradition.

First of all, our assigned table hosted two other American couples who were delightful. One couple, she of the cough too, and her retired police chief husband became good friends with us while sharing local restaurant recommendations. The other couple sported a beautiful woman wearing a lovely scarf—which gave me pause to always remember to pack a colorful scarf for dressy occasions—and her jovial husband, who was the manager of a most exclusive country club in Florida. Several tables—under, that is—housed beautifully trained dogs belonging to the guests. The evening began with a brief violin and piano concert of appropriate holiday music. Each guest was given a lovely menu stating the meal and proper wines to be served. From the red amaryllis table decorations to the finishing desert wine and signature soufflé, the event was pure elegance.

From the first frigid night I had spent in Rothenburg, where I fantasized spending Christmas there, to seventeen years later and actually realizing my dream, I shall always hold this particular

Christmas close to my heart. I would like to return for Christmas in Rothenburg, but Dad says perfection is difficult to repeat and I might be disappointed. He is probably correct.

You might think this is the end of the Christmas story. Wrong! Upon gathering our belongings to head to the airport and go home to thaw out in sunny Southern California, Dad asked what I was going to do with the *priceless* Christmas tree. He announced that security would never let me through carrying a tree with accompanying decorations. My response was, "WATCH ME!" There is nothing much like German heritage tenacity.

Friends, may I tell you that that little tree is decorated each year and stands in a place of honor in our home. It is a scrawny little tree much in the likes of Charlie Brown trees, but it holds treasured memories of happiness and love that can never be duplicated in a lifetime.

France

France is a beautiful country. Dad and I have not spent as much time there as we have and still do in Germany. But there is a special feeling one has when seeing the many vineyards, wandering through the museums, touring the vast palaces, and dining on superb cuisine while sipping the most perfect wines.

The people who live in the large cities such as Paris, Lyon, etc., can be quite snobbish and do not like it when tourists attempt to speak their native language. They can also look confused when one speaks English to them. My former French teacher, Dr. Hart, tells me that French folks have taken English in school, and they are just being uppity. Dad and I have found that many foreign countries like Americans to come and spend their money but are not too thrilled to deal with us as tourists. So Dad and I always try to be on our best behavior.

When one visits the villages, they will find sights, sounds, and smells unlike anywhere else on Earth—and these are good things. You will find the mustard fields around Dijon, the lavender fields of Haute-Provence, the heavy musk of grapes during the harvest, and art and history dating back to the Romans.

I cannot think of France without sharing with you a wonderful writer/author, Peter Mayle by name, who writes the most delightful and insightful books about France—mostly Provence. He documents the many problems in his quest to remodel a chateau and his association with workmen along the way.

Now back to our France. Dad and I managed to drive from one end of France to the other without getting too lost. However,

I did mention once to Dr. Hart that Dad and I had driven over Brenner's Pass and the Swiss Alps en route to France. She quickly responded that there are NO Swiss Alps. There are only French Alps, and they are called only ALPS.

Walk a Few Miles in My Shoes

Paris

France is an amazing country and Paris is the jewel. Dad and I have spent little time in Paris, as we prefer the welcoming arms of the French villages—well, sometimes welcoming as long as you speak their language *PERFECTLY*.

Most commercial flights take you to Charles de Gaulle Airport, where it is almost impossible for us to negotiate luggage, rental cars, etc., without Dad having a MAJOR ALTERCATION with some Frenchman, and in a foreign language, I might add. All the while, I am attempting to stuff Dad into said rental car without his being accosted by a deranged, arm-waving (maybe it was just one finger) male person with a *radioactive* personality. Do you know that well-known travel books have devoted complete sections describing how to arrive and exit Charles De Gaulle Airport? That, in and of itself, should explain the aforementioned trauma.

Once out of the airport (whew), we were on our way to, and yet, another little and old hotel across from the Louvre Museum. As Dad previously had litigation in Paris, he had located the lovely Hotel Regina. I remember one especially good evening there when we dined, fireside, on delicious cuisine. I chose lamb, and Dad had kidneys, *rein* a French word I quickly learned so that I would NEVER EVER order that for dinner.

One main reason for being in Paris for a few days was for Dad to meet with his French law associates. Upon reading the local French-written street map, Dad determined the associate's law office was an easy walk from the hotel, along the River Seine. What could be more romantic than a leisurely stroll along the river? As my map-reading capabilities had previously been tested in Germany with a score of D-, I was thrilled to have Dad as a navigator.

Clothed in my winter wool knit dress, designer HIGH-heel shoes, and full-length fur coat—don't panic, PETA people, it was a fake fur but rather handsome—we began our trek to the law office. It was a beautiful winter day—somewhat cold but with a lovely warm sunshine. The perspiration began to DRIP and the hairdo began to DROOP during our nine-hundred-mile march, mostly in circles I believe. It turned out that Dad's French map-reading skill was no better than my German map acuity.

Actually, I learned that there are many streets and addresses in a French city or village that have the same name and number. For example, if the address is 3235 Napoleon Street, there can be a 3235 Napoleon Street bis. The "bis" means that there is another house or business close by with the same address. Lots of luck!

It is a good thing that French folks eat their lunch late in the afternoon, as that is when we finally arrived at the associate's office. The law associate (minimal English) and his secretary (good English) decided we should join them for lunch, which usually lasts several hours, with good food and LOTS OF GOOD WINE!

Following another WALK, we arrived, somewhat bedraggled, at a delightful restaurant where we gave proper attention to the food and WINE. The associate and the secretary were pleasant hosts, and an afternoon was enjoyed by all. The main thing I remember about the feast is that the French people DO NOT USE BREAD PLATES. They simply put their scrumptious French rolls—crumbs and all—directly on the table cloth. I suppose that removes the mystery of where to place the salad plate, which is really no mystery at all, as in France it comes just before dessert. Full of great food and giddy from fine wine, Dad and I hailed a TAXI that gently delivered us back to the comfort of the Hotel Regina.

A few years later, Dad and I were again in Paris to meet with another law associate, as the previous associate had prematurely passed away. We somewhat successfully escaped De Gaulle Airport with just a little rise in blood pressure. Maybe we are getting better at this. Once rental-car-bound, we were on our way back to the familiar Hotel Regina.

I believe I have previously mentioned my French teacher, Dr. Hart, who, bless her soul, tried her best to at least teach me how to order from a menu and ask for a hotel room. Nearing the end of one of our sessions, Dr. Hart began to give me some interesting tidbits about Paris—thankfully in English—as she was beginning to get the message she had a challenged student on her hands.

Dr. Hart shared with me the story of Chateau de Malmaison, which is located about fifteen kilometers west of central Paris. Chateau de Malmaison was the home of the Empress Josephine and, from time to time, General Napoleon Bonaparte. So upon learning this chateau was in driving distance from the office of Dad's associate, I suggested we tour this palatial residence.

Now I should insert a character quirk of mine. I have always been fascinated with men who are small in stature with inferior backgrounds who have risen to great power—Napoleon and Adolph Hitler to name two. The personal stories of their ascent to hierarchy is still somewhat of a mystery to me. Perhaps, I am also historically challenged, as well as having a language glitch.

Armed with driving instructions given by the law associate and clutching a map, we were off in white-knuckle late-afternoon traffic to make our descent on Malmaison. Please don't forget that I am **MAP CHALLENGED** and therefore of little use.

All in all, we were driving along rather well, keeping up with the traffic flow and managing to ignore honking horns aimed toward our tourist driving acuity. Then we saw it in full frontal view—the ***ARC DE TRIOMPHE.*** Did you know that the Arc de Triomphe has, perhaps, fifty traffic lanes circling around at the speed of light, with many points shooting outward to heavily traveled streets? Well, fifty lanes may be a slight exaggeration, but to our minds, it certainly seemed that many.

With horns honking and whistle-blowing policemen frantically waving their arms, we finally made our entrance into one of the lanes. As it turned out, we had to maneuver our way across all the lanes and exit to a street directly opposite our initial entrance. So round and round we flew much in the fashion of a NASCAR driver at the Daytona 500. There are times when Dad is driving that I find it prudent to close my eyes and pray. And this was the time. Miracle of miracles, we managed to escape the jaws of the Arc de Triomphe traffic and find our way to Chateau Malmaison.

A bit of history, Josephine de Beauparnais bought the manor house in April 1797 for herself and her husband, General Napoleon Bonaparte, the future Napoleon I of France. Bonaparte expressed *fury* at Josephine for purchasing such an expensive house, for which she had paid well over three hundred thousand francs. The house needed extensive renovations, and she spent a fortune doing so.

According to some, Malmaison was the only place, next to a battlefield, where Napoleon could truly be himself. After their divorce, Josephine stayed on there, building up her superb rose garden and occasionally receiving visits from Emperor Napoleon, until her death in 1814. Napoleon returned and took residence in the house after his defeat at the Battle of Waterloo before his somewhat brief exile to the island of Saint Helena.

The next day, Dad and I spent the afternoon exploring the artist village of Montmartre. We enjoyed a delicious lunch at a rather bohemian cafe near the river Left Bank.

This brings back a memory of my previous trip to Paris and Montmartre. Along with three other young women (all in our early thirties), we were wandering down the narrow streets when we spied, through opened shutters, a chef making crepes. The chef became so *enthralled* with the four of us that he BURNED THE CREPES. With that, the chef slammed the shutter closed so to hide his embarrassment. It surely gave us a good chuckle.

The evening following our Malmaison adventure, Dad and I agreed that we both had visited Paris previously and had seen most of the tourist sites. With that in mind, we decided to leave Paris the next morning and wander down the road to begin our search, as usual, for a hotel for the night.

The Mighty House of Bling

Versailles

Yes, I have written about Versailles and the Chateau earlier. And the dinner in the Hall of Mirrors was extraordinary, to say the least. However, I do not often think of that particular event, for it is somewhat overshadowed by another trip Dad and I made one winter.

During one of our small dinner parties that included our world-traveling friend and client, Big M, Dad and I began to talk about our impending winter trip to France. Big M asked me where I stayed when I had previously visited Versailles. The answer was Paris—a bit away from Versailles. Big M then suggested Dad and I consider staying at the *GRAND TRIANON HOTEL,* now referred to as the *TRIANON PALACE,* as he believed that was the *ONLY* place to stay in Versailles.

The hotel sounded good to me and was located in easy walking distance to the Palace of Versailles. Not to be discouraged by the $$$$ signs in the travel guidebook, we proceeded to make reservations for a night or two. Though I haven't confirmed this, Big M said the Trianon Hotel served as a military post commanded by General Dwight D. Eisenhower during World War II.

After several days of work for Dad in Paris, we made the short drive to Versailles. Reservations in hand, we were shown to a room that was to die for. It was a beautiful corner room, housing a king-size bed with pink satin spread and comforter, sitting area, marble fireplace, and an elegant bathroom. Dad, who is the *king of naps,* proceeded directly to the bed while I decided to enjoy a bath of elixirs for the body (bubbles and sweet-smelling bath salts).

As I bundled into my luxurious hotel-furnished bathrobe, I noticed the sun was beginning to set. Immediately, I was aware that there was a direct correlation between the setting sun and the temperature in the room. Our beautiful corner room, with large windows on two sides, quickly became a room in which one could hang meat for a family of six for the entire winter. With Dad and me both shivering seismically under the covers, Dad managed to phone the desk and ask for help. Sure enough, just like $$$$ hotels advertise, an attendant quickly arrived to regulate the heat. Now, friend, let me tell you, this hotel was built in 1910, abused a bit by the war, and was only cosmetically upgraded. The heat adjustment helped some but certainly not enough to relax in the sitting area and have a sip of wine—that is, without getting frostbite on our noses and an overchill to the wine.

Dad and I decided in order to survive, we should dress and go downstairs for a light supper and a beverage or two, thinking the ingestion of food and alcohol might help to warm the body. We were able to find a small bar off the lobby that served good wine and a small repast. But this was not the best part—***IN NO WAY.***

The best part was a drama composed of a couple, one of whom, the female, was celebrating her birthday. Never in my life have I seen such a display of multiple expensive gifts. The scene plays out this way. The male suitor presents a gift of supreme good taste and cost—for example, a Louis Vuitton handbag for which he expects a juicy kiss in return. Then the birthday girl orders a whiskey drink for both of them, whereby only *HE* drinks and she does not. Next comes a silk Hermes scarf. A juicy kiss follows and another whiskey for him. Following the imbibing of more whiskey, another extravagant gift is presented—a diamond necklace. Another juicy kiss and another drink for him as she awaits another gift and so on. This scenario continues for many gifts and many drinks. Here,

I must add that after each drink, the suitor slipped lower and lower on the love seat until he no longer could function normally or, possible, not at all.

As a famous radio announcer used to say, "Now, for the rest of the story . . ." The hotel attendants half carried, half dragged the suitor to his room; the birthday girl made out with fabulous loot; and the suitor woke up the next morning with a tremendous headache, money lost, and, most importantly, **ALONE.** Moral of the story is that the suitor had a mission to accomplish, and the birthday girl had a somewhat different mission. So don't ever count out the larceny of a female who is celebrating her birthday. To this day, this is one of our favorite travel stories, which makes us laugh every time.

Before leaving Versailles the next morning, we decided to briefly tour the Chateau de Versailles. The palace is possibly the most gilded architectural *bling* in existence. And King Louis XIV slightly rivals Crazy King Ludwig of Germany in their palace/castle extravagance. King Louis XIV championed the partial construction of Chateau de Versailles and Chateau de Fontainebleau, whereas Crazy King Ludwig **MYSTERIOUSLY** died during a midnight boating accident, perhaps for his castle extravagence

When touring the Chateau de Versailles, one has the dubious pleasure of walking shoulder to shoulder among a herd of tourists. The chateau is forever crowded. We did notice that in order to avoid the tour bus onslaught, one should tour during the lunch hour. Around noontime, the buses load up and schlep the "*health shoes*" tourists off to the local greasy spoon—that is, if there is anything such as a greasy spoon in France (the French are known for their food, as well as their wine).

Dad and I agreed that due to the frigid hotel, plus the apparent tourist migration, which is only rivaled by the famous wildebeest migration in Africa, we would wander down the roadway and escape to one of Dad's favorite villages, Fontainebleau.

Do Palace Dogs Pee in the Fountain?

Fontainebleau

Fontainebleau, a mere thirty-eight miles southeast of Paris, is one of Dad's favorite villages. The palace there is one of the Renaissance period, as opposed to Versailles, which is of the baroque style with lots of *froufrou*. The trip to Fontainebleau is an easy day trip from Paris, and Dad and I toured and stayed for two nights.

The Chateau de Fontainebleau served as a retreat and hunting lodge beginning in the sixteenth century, although additions were made for the next three hundred years. Residents of note were Marie Antoinette and Pope Pius VII, who arrived in June of 1812, accompanied by his personal physician. In poor health, the pope was the prisoner of Napoleon and remained there for nineteen months. All in all, thirty-four sovereigns from Louis VI to Napoleon III spent time in Fontainebleau.

The Palace of Fontainebleau is perhaps Dad's favorite palace. Upon touring the palace, I found beautiful restorations and furnishings. All the important rooms were there for me—Josephine's bedroom, Napoleon's apartment and bedroom—where I was told Napoleon really did sleep in that bed—and the throne room.

But there were two things that stood out in Dad's memory as *points of interest*. One was a walkway (mall) that featured a half-size replica of the Washington Monument and the mall in DC. Dad often wondered if the Washington Monument architecture was copied. The other—and I guess it is a MAN THING—is a gateway fountain sporting a horse-head statuary spitting water into the pond, accompanied by hunting-dog-type statues *making PEE-PEE* in the water. The interesting thing is that in my research I can find no mention of the mall/structure or the dog fountain. But guess what, I have seen photographs of the mall and have actually seen the naughty dogs performing their deed. Maybe the French are not too proud of these particular works of art.

I suppose the one thing that stood out in my mind was the famous horseshoe staircase that dominates the Cour du Cheval Blanc (White Horse Courtyard). It was down this staircase that Napoleon made his way to receive a final salute from his Old Guard (Vieille Garde) shortly before his first abdication in 1814. The courtyard has since been named the Courtyard of Goodbyes.

The forest surrounding the city of Fountebleau is a former royal hunting park. It is open, to this day, for hikers, horse riders, and rock climbers.

And one final bit of information and perhaps the most interesting piece of all is that the European campus of the INSEAD business school is located at the edge of Fontainebleau. In 2011, INSEAD ranked as the *Bloomberg Businessweek*'s number one international business school, *Forbes*'s number one for ROI, and *Financial Times* 2011's number four business school in the world.

Got Mustard?

Beaune

Driving along the Alps on our way to Pforzheim, Germany, Dad and I spied a sign reading *Beaune.* Dad's often-mentioned client, Big M, had told us about the charming village of Beaune and its prominent place in the Burgundy wine region of France. Realizing Beaune was only a few miles out of the way to Pforzheim, we decided to pay it a brief visit.

Since it was nearing the noon hour in Beaune, we decided to park our car and venture into the village for a bite to eat. On a corner we found a tiny *brasserie* with three small tables and a stairway leading down to a warm and friendly *cave.* As we were still doing our major European travel during the winter months, we were almost frozen stiff, and the cave spewing delicious aromas lured us right in. At this point, I should say Dad has driven across entire countries to eat a special meal. For example, he loves sausage and sauerkraut in Garmisch, spaghetti carbonara in Sienna, and wild mushroom soup in Oberammergau; so this gastronomic detour to Beaune was no surprise to me. Following a delectable meal of steaming French onion soup, freshly baked crusty bread, and a glass of the local burgundy wine, we decided we would return to Beaune when finishing our business in Pforzheim. And so we did.

Oh by the way, Dad and I were on our way to Pforzheim for a meeting with Dad's German law associate, Ulrich, who lived there. This is the same Ulrich, of the skinny leather pants, who often met us in Munich. Ulrich invited us to lunch, where he *insisted* we partake of the canapés. Being a good sport, I *woofed* down several only to discover I had eaten *RABBIT.* This was most shocking, as I am an avid domestic animal lover.

Returning to Beaune on the weekend with no hotel reservations became a bit of a problem. We finally found a room, or more likely a converted cleaning closet. Not to worry, as our crosshairs were on the local *brasserie* where we had eaten two days previously. Braving the bitter cold and making mental landmarks so that we wouldn't spend the night LOST, as we often were, we made our way to the *cave.* Again, a tasty meal was served and devoured. An especially good mustard accompanied our repast, and as we were in the heart of the Dijon region, we decided to purchase some to take home with us.

The next morning we, again, went to the brasserie to ask the name of the mustard that was served the night before. Remember, friends, no French here and no English there. First of all the waiter with whom we spoke thought we were complaining about the mustard and seemed most offended. I shook my head NO and followed with a hands-to-lips smiley face. The waiter somehow got the message and wrote the name of the mustard on a small piece of paper.

Having spied a mustard and wine shop within walking distance, we scurried along to make our purchase of mustard, wine, and a corkscrew—no screw-top bottles there. Also, one might be shot if wine in a box were found on the premises. The shopkeeper was most solicitous and began to show us different gourmet mustards that would travel well to the United States. We found a wonderful corkscrew made of an old varnished grapevine, along with a nice selection of wine for hotel room sipping. After a bit of *search* and *rescue* for the tiny paper in the black well of my purse, I asked the shopkeeper if he had any Amore in his shop. The shopkeeper spun around, turned up his nose, and quickly stomped away. As he continued to ignore us, we felt fortunate to snatch his attention long enough to pay for and escape with the corkscrew.

Upon our return home and during one of my ill-fated French lessons with Dr. Hart, I asked if she were familiar with the mustard AMORE. Indeed she was. It turned out that Amore is the equivalent of FRENCH'S mustard in the good old United States. No wonder the prissy shopkeeper wanted nothing more to do with us classless Americans. When revisiting Beaune, Dad and I shopped at the local grocery market and were privy to purchase as much Amore as we could *schlep* back on the airplane in a suitcase.

As I have said, available hotel rooms in Beaune on the weekend are scarce, to say the least. The village follows the old European custom where young people from outlying areas come together for parties, which *stagger* well into the night. However, signs for a hotel chain, HOTEL-DIEU, seemed to appear with regularity in French villages—somewhat like Holiday Inn or Motel 6 at home. And in Beaune, it is advertised that wine tastings occur in the Hotel-Dieu. Well, watch out, folks, here we come.

May I suggest that before traveling to France, that it is highly recommended for one to take along an English/French dictionary, as it turns out that the illusive Hotel-Dieu is actually a hospital or hospice. In fact, some of the finest vineyards are owned by the Hospices de Beaune (Hotel-Dieu). Founded in 1943, the Hospice de Beaune carried on its medical activities until 1971, with its nurses still sporting their strange medieval uniforms. The hospital was founded as a free hospital and has a reliable income stemming from its 143-acre vineyard. A visit to the hospice is a highlight of any visit to Beaune.

Beaune is all about wine. There are vineyards stretching both north and south. Driving north, one will find Nuits-Saint-George, where wine has been made since Roman times. It is said that this wine was recommended to Louis XIV for medicinal use. Well, I'll sip to that. Also driving north, you will find Chateau du Clos de Vouget, constructed in the twelfth century and is the home of Burgundy's exclusive company of wine lovers, the Confrerie des Chevaliers du

Tastevin. This group gathers there in November at the start of an annual three-day festival, the TROIS GLORIEUSES.

Traveling south from Beaune, you will soon pass through Pommard, Volnay, and Meursault before continuing on to Chassagne-Montrachet. Vast vineyards, with tasting rooms found in the villages, surround each of these areas. You can purchase wine at a fairly decent price if you buy it from an individual producer.

Finding December a bit frigid and difficult for auto travel, Dad and I made subsequent trips to Beaune in the fall. There is almost nothing to compare with the riot of color you will find in the vineyards, with the leaves turning brilliant red, orange, and gold. In September, you might be lucky enough to arrive during the grape harvest. Entire families from surrounding villages move from one vineyard to another, harvesting the grapes by hand and depositing them into baskets hung on their backs. While the men carry the not-too-big grape baskets, the women stoop, kneel, crawl, and stretch to clip the bunches. The baskets then are emptied into wagons pulled by tractors that are then driven into Beaune to the presses. With the women getting the more labor intensive of the harvest chores, I decided, then, I wanted nothing to do with grapes other than sipping fine red wine from a crystal goblet.

This brings back a memory of my trip to Spain with friend Ida Jo. There we witnessed the harvest of olives. The men stood under the olive trees, bopping the tree branches with a long stick, while the women worked on their hands and knees to pick up the fallen olives. It was then I decided I wanted nothing to do with olives, other than their floating in a martini glass.

But back to the harvest. During the harvest, there is a euphoric scent of grape musk throughout the entire village. Small villages might give you a glimpse of family life, where harvested grapes are dumped into antique wooden presses and then raked and stomped by children—somewhat like LUCY AND ETHEL did in their iconic TV show past.

Releasing the Beaujolais nouveau each year is an event anticipated by the whole village. One of the most frivolous and animated rituals in the wine world has begun. It has become a worldwide race to be the first to serve this new wine, and in doing so, it will be carried by motorcycles, balloons, trucks, helicopters, jets, elephants, runners, and rickshaws to get it to its final destination. At one minute past midnight on the third Thursday of each November, from little villages and towns, cases of Beaujolais nouveau begin their journey through a sleeping France to Paris for immediate shipment to all parts of the world. Rows of the new Beaujolais wine crowd market shelves, only to be released at the given day and time all over the world. When released, the wine is ready for drinking. The race from grape to glass may be silly, but half the fun is knowing that on the same night, in homes, cafes, restaurants, pubs, bars, and bistros around the world, the same celebration is taking place.

I don't believe in reincarnation, for if I did, I'm certain I would remember something of my past. However, the first and subsequent times I was in Beaune among the vast vineyards, I had a feeling I had been there before. This extreme sensation took over my power of good sense and told me that we should plant a vineyard at our home in Fallbrook. And so we did.

Shortly after planting, watering, grafting, and spraying seven acres of *little sticks,* I began to realize why wine cost a bit more than a diet soda and is certainly more labor intensive. If you ever need to "scratch the itch for your personal vineyard," take a trip to Beaune, let the others tend to the vines, and all you have to do is sit back and sip the fruit of their labors.

Hotel de Ville

Arles

It's difficult to know where to begin my story about Arles. First of all, for you art lovers, Arles was the somewhat brief home of Vincent van Gogh. In fact, Arles was where van Gogh wielded the knife (historians believe) that removed the left lobe of his ear in homage to the artist Gauguin, whom he had come to idolize. This was much like a matador who presents (to his lady love) an ear from a dispatched bull. Others have said that van Gogh removed his ear due to a constant ringing in his ears, while still others lament that the procedure was done to cure an ear infection.

Enough history for the moment. This is New Year's Eve, and Dad and I are driving late afternoon in pursuit of a hotel for the night. Remember Dad's penchant for NO reservations. Having previously spent one or two New Year's Eves in Germany, we remembered that all stores and markets close around noon and do not reopen for several days.

Approaching St. Tropez, we decided to stop and buy some bread and cheese so we would have provisions for the evening. Sprinting through St. Tropez, at Olympic trial speed, we found a market, crowded it was, and bought what little there was left. Apparently, the French folks also knew there would be no shopping for a while.

Once back on the road, driving through Provence and the beautiful chateaus and vineyards, I began to get my usual dose of late afternoon *PANIC* regarding our lack of a hotel room for the night. Spying a sign reading ARLES, Dad suggested we drive through to see what hotels might be available.

Arriving in the village, we spotted a *VERY* familiar hotel sign, **HOTEL DE VILLE.** We had seen identical signs in almost every French village we had visited. **OBVIOUSLY,** this was an important hotel chain similar to Holiday Inn in the United States. As my *map-reading skill* was not an option, we began to follow directional signs through the town. And there were plenty. Turn right here, turn left there, go around the block, parking nearby, etc. But, friends, there was no hotel to be seen, and we had done this before while looking for the elusive Hotel de Ville in other French villages. What kind of a French *trick* was this?? These hotels are **EVERYWHERE** in France, but we can never seem to actually locate one. It was sometime later, when, during my French lesson with Dr. Hart, I learned Hotel de Ville was the **TOWN HALL**; and of course, it could be found in every French city and village. I've often wondered if the French did that just to aggravate the Americans.

Having given up on finding the mysterious Hotel de Ville, we seriously began our hotel search. Voila! We did find a rather charming hotel where we could stay for a day or two. Our country French room contained an adequate bathroom, television, and king-size bed. We were lucky, indeed.

Once situated, we decided to take a stroll and wander the ancient narrow and twisting streets home to small shops and restaurants. As the dinner hour was approaching, at least the American dinner (the Europeans dine much later), Dad and I spied a small and charming restaurant. Upon entering, we were told, "Yes, you may come in for dinner." We dined on roast duck and lamb, along with a bottle of fine red wine—a gastronomical excellence. The stale bread and cheese of St. Tropez was now a distant memory.

Upon leaving the restaurant, we apparently made an incorrect turn, as we began to WANDER where nothing looked familiar.

The narrow and twisting streets, pedestrian only, were almost void of people. One young woman passed by, and we asked her the directions to McDonald's of the Arches. Surely this woman understood the word "McDonald's," even though she did not speak English. Well, for goodness' sake, there was even a small sign on the corner that posted a picture of the McDonald's clown, and the woman just stood there and shook her head. THANKS! By the way, the reason we were on the trail to McDonald's was that it was directly across the street from our hotel. So more wandering we did in pursuit of other McDonald's signs—and there were precious few. In fact, the precious few eventually became nonexistent.

Dad and I walked for hours on end, or so it seemed, turning, twirling, and twisting in the cold and drizzle, when finally we staggered, miraculously, onto the main street on which our hotel was located, all be it about two miles downstream. Stumbling into the hotel, we decided that all in all it had been a festive New Year's Eve, and because of the rain, there were no fireworks to keep us awake all night.

On a bright and sunny New Year's morning, Dad and I decided to stay an extra day in Arles. I had learned, in my travel book, there was an arena that was built in the first century AD to seat twenty-one thousand people. In the middle ages, it was plundered to resemble more a feudal fortification than a sports arena. Complete restoration began in 1825, and today it is used primarily for the spectacle of bullfights. Only the arena in Nimes is better preserved. We also learned that van Gogh's famous painting, *Maison Jaune* (*The Yellow House*), was the house in Arles where he lived for a time. Unfortunately, the house was demolished during World War II.

Our Arles New Year's Eve experience proved to be so successful we resolved to do a repeat performance the next year. This time I (Mom), in full plan-ahead mode, would go into travel action with proper reservations. Long-distance calling with poor phone connections, plus a FOREIGN LANGUAGE, ***FRENCH***, was due cause to put on my worry hat. Oh well, nothing ventured, nothing blah, blah, blah. Also, I believe the reservation clerk in Arles had never heard the word "CONFIRMATION," and perhaps "RESERVATION" as well.

So in we walked asking for our *hopefully* familiar hotel room of the previous year. Not only did they not have our previous room, but they also had never heard of us. In addition, there was no dining facility available, as the hotel was hosting a private **SILVESTER.** Sweet Lord, the wrath of the Germans had leaked over into France, as New Year Silvesters were a tradition of Germany.

The clerk scrambled around and found one room that we could have. Let's have a look. There we found two scrimpy beds, one wooden chair, and a small but fairly efficient bathroom. It was located on the ground floor, directly across from the infamous Silvester-to-be. This would not do! Dad and I both verbally attacked the clerk, along with a good bit of arm flapping. Finally, the snippy clerk gave up and gave us a room equivalent to our room of the former year. I have no idea who got stuck with the prison room, but frankly, Ms. Scarlett, I don't give a damn.

As late afternoon was now on us, Dad and I decided to walk to the charming restaurant where we enjoyed our New Year's Eve dinner the year before. We were certain we could find it, as that was not a problem last year. The problem was our inability to find our way back to the hotel. This year we would carefully mark our way to and from the café. With the restaurant in our sights, we began to speculate on what we would order for our New Year's festivity and of course which wine we would choose for accompaniment. WHAT'S THIS! A sign in our warm and fuzzy restaurant stated that it would be hosting a Silvester and was sold out. **HOW CAN THAT BE**!

Releasing our fear of becoming totally lost, as in the previous year, we set out in pursuit of another eating establishment. This became a high priority, as we had arrived in Arles without provisions, and night was soon to be on us along with the now familiar French drizzle and cold. Whoever said this "seek and ye shall find" business was full of cotton stuffing. We did seek and WE DID NOT FIND. The good news is that we did not get completely lost—just a little bit. So back we trudged to the hotel to surrender to the in-house Silvester. Guess what? SOLD OUT! This was not looking good. Cold, rain, no prepurchased provisions, and no Silvester. What kind of New Year's Eve celebration was this?

Aha! Good old Dad to the rescue. Remembering that McDonald's was just across the street from our hotel, he sprang into action, and in just the right time, I might add. As the attendants were beginning their closing chores, Dad wedged his way through the partially closed door and placed his order for two Big Macs and fries.

So there we were, sitting in bed, eating burgers and fries, listening to the gentle rainfall and watching French TV. All in all, a most memorable New Year's Eve!

Riots and Croissants

Carcassonne

I have absolutely no idea why we decided to travel to Carcassonne, but we were en route to Alecante, Spain, and Carcassone was on our way. Also, I thought it might be a great place to spend my birthday. Still, I don't remember the reason why this became such an important issue in my life. Boy, am I glad it did!

Carcassonne, a beautiful medieval city, is divided in half by the longest city walls in Europe. The fortified upper half is known as la Cite. The lower half is simply known as Carcassonne. Unless you are staying in the upper town, you are not allowed to bring your car. Carcassonne is located in the Languedoc-Roussillon region, which extends along the southern Mediterranean coast of France to the Pyrenees. The inland area of the region is virtually one huge vineyard, with perfectly pruned vines dressed in the winter snow.

One last bit of history that is truly fascinating is the story of Charlemagne, who once set siege to the settlement in the ninth century. Dame Carcas, an extremely creative and cleaver woman, boldly fed the last of the city's wheat to a pig in full view of the conqueror. Charlemagne, believing the town had an endless supply of food, promptly closed his camp and left. The townspeople were so thrilled with the victory they named the town Carcassonne in honor of Dame Carcas.

The Hotel de la Cite, where we stayed, hosted few guests, as it was in the dead of winter with a possible snowstorm on the way.

After settling, we decided to explore the village to find a restaurant suitable for my birthday feast. Finding few restaurants open during the winter off-season, we spied a warm country French brasserie filled with smiling guests. We agreed, this is the place (much like Brigham Young exclaimed upon finding what is now known as Salt Lake City). We were seated at a small table surrounded by French-speaking diners. Oh my, the food on others' plates looked scrumptious. We soon discovered there were no English menus similar to what we found in Germany. Not to worry. My many lessons with the oft-mentioned Dr. Hart would certainly come into action. When perusing the menu, it quickly came to my attention that I had *no idea* what the printed word said. Again, not to worry. In my very best Dr. Hart—taught French, I proceeded to order a meal located somewhere in my personal Dr. Hart memory bank.

The prissy waiter with small hips and fluffy coiffed hair appeared not to understand one word of my Southern-accented French. After trying several times to communicate with Mr. Prissy, guests at the adjoining table offered their help. The chain of translation went something like my English to the guest, their French to Mr. Prissy, and Mr. Prissy to the kitchen chef. After several minutes, Mr. Prissy returned with his hands flapping in the air. Obviously, there was a communication breakdown somewhere. I began to sense there might be a *riot* on the horizon. As there is no safe meal in France equal to Wiener schnitzel in Germany, I simply used hand signals to show that we would have what the people at the next table were having. All ended well. The next table people were happy we chose their meal, our dinner was delicious, and Mr. Prissy thought he had won the battle of languages.

Awakening very early the next morning, we decided to have a quick cup of coffee (hot chocolate for me) and perhaps a pastry of sorts prior to our leaving for Spain. Bundling up in our heavy winter coats, we were off to find the village café we had seen the day before. We remembered noticing a lady making the most delicious looking pastries, and we were on her trail for a sample or two. We found the lady, barely out of her warm bed, just beginning her morning baking ritual. She suggested we go across the street where her son and daughter would serve us coffee and chocolate. Moving across the street with the pastry lady, she walked up handmade wooden stairs to awaken her family to start the service of coffee. Pastry lady went back to her shop where she then made the most fabulous hot croissants, served with soft European butter. These, she brought back for us to have with our morning beverages. To this day, the thought of the hot homemade croissants and butter will put at least one pound on each hip—but certainly worth the memory.

Spain

My introduction to Spain was with my friend Ida Jo, when we made our "country club" tour with friends. We first landed in Madrid, which is a beautiful city, boasting of the Prado Museum and world-class bullfighting. Unfortunately, the "world-class" matadors had retired for the season (the previous week) and thus we were *treated* to novices. YOU DO NOT WANT TO BE TREATED TO NOVICES! With stadium seats VERY close to the arena, we could literally hear the blood drop from the bull, so we quickly retreated to the comforting arms of the hotel tapas bar.

One thing about being on a guided tour is that when one gets the hotel bartenders *trained* as to the kind of beverages and tapas the guests prefer, the tour leaves that location only to, again, find the need to *train* bartenders at a different hotel. (Also, the tour guides request that your luggage be placed outside your room for pickup at 6:30 a.m., which is cruel and inhuman treatment).

Tour bus conversations are fun on which to eavesdrop. I swear I heard that some of the tourists were going to see the ***flamingo*** dancers. Really, did they mean ***FLAMENCO*** dancers? Also, I am certain we overheard one of the tourists negotiate, with a street vendor, the purchase of a pair of *kitchenettes.* Could they possibly have been trying to buy a pair of *castanets,* a local souvenir favorite? These remarks came mostly from the Velcro-fastened, health-shoe generation. Ida and I purchased a pair of ***kitchenettes*** that we thought would make great ornaments for our Christmas trees at home. By the way, I still have mine, which hang prominently on my tree annually. In our newly acquired tour bus language, Ida and I clutched our *kitchenette* purchases and trotted off to watch the *flamingos* dance.

Our tour bused us down the Costa del Sol, where we stopped for a day or two in Malaga. In that area, the sun never seems to *set.* In late afternoon, Ida and I would share a bottle of wine on the beach where our "country club" companions would, one by one, stroll by and stop for a visit. Ida and I referred to this as *holding court.* Later our favorite subject of conversation was to debate who *had class and who did not.* We decided that money had nothing to do with *class*, and truly it does not. However, we did agree that some folks *scrubbed up* better than others.

One of the most astonishing sights, as I recall, was the plethora of *beach-bound* women baring their breasts during the *ritual* of sunbathing. Friends, let me tell you, most of those I saw should not have bared their bosoms under any condition, and many should not have been in swimsuit attire (at least not in public view). I learned quickly that the expression *"cute and perky"* stops at about age twenty-five—which is when *serious gravity or droop and sag* takes over for the rest of your life.

I have shared with you a bit of Spain, where I traveled prior to my adventures with Dad. However, sometime later, Dad showed me a new and different Spain, mostly along the coast, where we searched for warm weather during our winter travels. We have not spent as much time in Spain as we have in Germany or France, but we loved our joyous times there.

PS. It also helps that I speak some Tex-Mex Spanish, even though the Spaniards speak Castellano (Castilian Spanish) with a pronounced *lisp.* Did you know that many, many years ago, the king of Spain spoke with a lisp, and therefore, all of his countrymen were likewise ordered to speak with a lisp so as not to embarrass him? For example, "GRATHIUS," not "GRACIAS."

The Party Animals Are Here

Barcelona

Barcelona is a two-thousand-year-old city and was the capital of Catalonia until Madrid became the seat of the royal court in 1561. Barcelona is one of Europe's most visually beautiful cities and has long rivaled Madrid, both economically and politically.

Dad and I spent only about twenty-four hours in Barcelona, which made it a short-lived New Year's Eve celebration. By the time we found our way to the local Ritz Carlton Hotel and settled ourselves—a really special room rate was found for us by our favorite travel agent, Carol—it was time for cocktails and dinner. We decided to check on the complementary concierge repast and were delightfully surprised. There were food and beverages fit for any dining guest. So party animals that we are (ha), we ate a bit, sipped a bit, and were in bed well before midnight.

The next morning, Dad, the early riser, left on a walk around the hotel area while I attempted to gather myself to leave for unknown adventures down the road. Within a very few minutes, Dad was back at the door saying I must go outside to see what had taken place New Year's Eve night. First let me say our hotel was very quiet, with no sounds of fireworks or loud music. So I was shocked to find, across the street from the hotel, approximately ten enormous white tents, each containing loud music, rivers of alcoholic beverages, and throngs of young humanity dancing wildly. This was 10:00 a.m. and had been going on for who knows how long. There, I truly found the accurate definition of "party animals."

Barcelona is full of spectacular sights for all to see. There are churches, museums, superb food markets, and excellent restaurants. There are beaches and promenades. There is even a monument of Christopher Columbus marking the spot where he stepped back onto Spanish soil in 1493 after discovering America. Did we see any of these wonderful sights? No, not even one! As this trip was taken during the days of our driving the whole day while looking for a bed for the night (instead of spending time sightseeing the area), we left Barcelona with a promise to one day return.

From Dad's map, it appeared that Tossa de Mar might be our next destination.

Turn Left, Now!

Tossa de Mar

Tossa de Mar is located on the Costa Brava (Wild Coast) and was christened "Blue Paradise" by painter Marc Chagall, who summered there for four decades. Tossa is a walled medieval town and boasts pristine beaches, which are among Catalonia's best. Surrounding the old town are medieval walls and towers dating back to the twelfth century. On a promontory jutting out into the sea, the many towers, which are a local pride and joy, give a glance into a fortified town and are the only examples of such on the entire Catalan coast.

Dad and I, with camera swinging from my neck, trudged up the hill in order to see the towers firsthand and to enjoy the coastal view from above. After a brief rest, we decided it would be prudent to wind our way down the hill in order to find a bed for the night.

Old town Tossa is a burrow of very steep, narrow cobblestone streets, with many restored buildings—all of which look curiously alike. As this was New Year's Day, many of the hotel clerks showed "wear" from the previous late night and preferred not to be disturbed with new guests. We were shown one room with two barrack-type beds/cots and paper-thin walls. It was reminiscent of the *prison room* we were shown in Arles some years previous.

Our decision was to go down the road in hopes of finding a better inn for the night. If only we could locate the car, which we parked several hours earlier. Not only did most of the buildings look alike, which allowed for no landmark identification, the streets were a mass of look-alike confusion. So up, down, and all around we walked. Finally, spotting our trusty rental car, we began our journey for a bed for the night. The roads were somewhat remote and towns were rather far apart and it was getting dark outside. We began to think the "prison" bed in Tossa might have been a good choice.

As our feathers began to droop and the night got darker, I began to get a bit panicky. About that time, we spied a large white stucco building with a lighted sign reading ***escuela hotel—OPEN.*** Even in my Tex-Mex Spanish, I knew that the sign stated this was a hotel school and was open for business. In my usual quiet and refined way, I yelled, "Go left, **NOW**, Dad." And so he did.

Once inside, we discovered we had found a pure treasure. The staff spoke English, which was a great help. It appeared we were the only guests, and the many students who were on site were quick to answer any of our needs. The beautiful dining room, with fine linens and fresh flowers, had several waiters in tux and more than one chef with a big white hat. All were watched over by, I presume, a *food-meister* of some sort, and he was quick to correct any of the staff, if necessary. The menu was extensive and the food delicious. Our bedroom was not lavish but impeccably clean. This brings to mind the saying "Even a blind hog finds an acorn," and we truly had found the acorn.

The next morning found Dad wanting to drive to Valencia for the day and perhaps a night. Bidding our friendly hotel *adios*, we began our trek to Valencia. The only thing I knew about Valencia was *oranges*. And sure enough there they were, fields of orange trees—one after the other. As Dad and I live on a ranch with a rather large orange grove, we decided the city of Valencia was probably not a place of interest for us—even though we noted the trees were beautifully trimmed and topped, something we should work on at home. So in Dad's usual driving mode, he made a rapid

U-turn back toward our place of origin. I refer to this as an origin, as I have no clue as to where the hotel school was actually located. It was just *there* on the road by itself. So drive we did *in the dark.*

Somehow, nothing looked familiar. Finally seeing a service station, we stopped and Dad said that I should get out and ask for directions back to the main road. It was then I realized my Tex-Mex Spanish bore little or no resemblance to the language spoken in Spain. The station attendant began to wave his arms and usually in one direction. Dad and I decided we should drive in the general area where the arms were pointing. For about an hour, we drove, in pitch-black dark, on a narrow and winding road with tall thick forest on either side. There were no other cars either coming or going and no moon to light the night. This time I felt we were truly on the *devil's highway.* I suspected we were terribly lost when later I spied a faint light on a white stucco tower proclaiming the existence of the **escuela hotel.**

"DAD, TURN LEFT, NOW!"

Do you believe in *ANGELS*? Well, believe me, I do. The angels gently delivered us back to the hotel school and to the waiting arms of the student staff.

The Paella Was Black

Alicante

Ah, Alicante. Our Alicante trip was made during the height of winter and was especially for Dad to meet with a law associate who had recently relocated from London. Much like our trip to Barcelona, there were museums, cathedrals, basilica, a *drop-dead* beautiful esplanade lined with date palm trees, and, of course, the Castle Santa Barbara, which looms high over the city. But like Barcellona, we did not see any of these tourist relics. However, our hotel was located on a lovely beach, which teems with wall-to-wall people during the summer.

For some strange reason, several of Dad's foreign associates were a bit quirky (some more than others). One particular associate named Clark insisted, apparently, on bringing a bit of Great Britain with him to Alicante. This included his extremely rude and disconnected wife and two sons who were well on their way to a life of delinquency. However, Clark's principal British attachment was his *full-size Range Rover* automobile.

When researching, I discovered that the surrounding areas of Alicante were (can you believe this) seven thousand years old. Now I'm certain the streets had been rebuilt, somewhat, in the last seven thousand years; but let me tell you, they are still *NARROW*. So good ole Clark in his full-size Range Rover took both sides of the street while maneuvering us through the city. He actually used the middle street line to center his car—much like an airplane pilot does on the runway when taking off and landing. Also, finding a parking place big enough was next to impossible for the oversized *beast* of an automobile. Climbing in and getting out of the *beast* proved to be extremely difficult for my five-foot, two-inch body with short legs. Wearing a *pencil-slim* skirt and high-heel shoes on the auto ascent gave passersby full view of what used to be my modesty.

Clark had a delightful secretary/associate who joined us and Clark's dysfunctional family for lunch at a restaurant known for their paella. Clark—does this remind you of Clark Griswold (Chevy Chase) of the *National Lampoon* movies?—whose command of the Spanish language was no better than his driving acuity, insisted on ordering lunch for the lot of us. I did recognize a few of his words such as *pollo* (chicken), *conejo* (rabbit), and *arroz* (rice). Clark stumbled and mumbled in *pigeon Spanish* until Carolina, secretary/associate and native Spaniard, took over the menu task, and well she did. Poor Clark, he truly wanted to project his *machoism.*

Carolina allowed that her mother cooked paella every Sunday and would only eat paella at this particular restaurant when dining out. When our paella was served, it bothered me not that some was traditional yellow, some red, and some black. The black worried me a bit when I found out the color was the result of squid ink as an ingredient. Bottom line, it was the best paella I have ever tasted, and Dad agreed as well.

Safely, back at our hotel, Dad and I learned there was a winter snowstorm on the way. As Alicante is located at the most southern part of Spain and our eventual departure for the United States was Paris, we decided to make a *run* for it before the storm arrived.

Making our way back to Beaune, our intermittent stop before Paris, was the most frightening drive we had ever made—including the United States. Following a convoy of large trucks, wet snow began to fall rather heavily. The backsplash from the trucks kept our windshield covered with mud. In short time, our windshield cleaning fluid was depleted. It was definitely time to pray. This continued for several dangerous hours. Finally, in the far distance, we spotted the dim lights of Beaune. Yes, God is good, and by the way, thanks for the angel too.

Back in our favorite Beaune hotel, we agreed that all future trips to Europe should be made in the fall and we should leave the winter holidays to Hawaii. And we have done so.

Songs of the Midnight Tenor

San Sebastian

San Sebastian has long been a favorite city of Dad's, and we have visited there several times. The city is located on one of the finest beaches (La Concha) in the world and is on par with Nice and Monte Carlo. As Dad and I traveled there in the winter months, we never experienced the local beach life. However, as San Sebastian is very near the French border, vacationers from France descend in droves during the summer, which has caused it to become one of the most expensive cities in Spain.

As Dad explained to me early on in our marriage that some hotels on the edge of town are better than others, we would experience varieties of these in our adventures. Remembering the guidebook description as "most expensive city," I was thrilled and surprised when Dad pulled in front of the beautiful Maria Cristina Hotel, which is reputedly the most expensive hotel in San Sebastian. This hotel on the edge of town was definitely one of the better ones. The guidebook even has stars beside the name. And heaven knows that *stars* and $$$$ are important when traveling.

"Old town" San Sebastian is an easy walking distance from the hotel—that is, if you turn the *right* way. It is brimming with tapas bars and inviting restaurants displaying fresh fish (of all classes) in the windows, may I repeat, if you turn the right way.

Speaking of the *right* way, one dark evening Dad and I decided to stroll to "old town" to locate a restaurant for dinner. Our stroll turned into something similar to the *Bataan Death March*, as we circled over bridges, walked between buildings (all this in nonwalking shoes, mind you), and ended our journey on the banks of an unknown river. Finally, Dad said he believed we had turned the *wrong* way when leaving the hotel. And yes, we had!

Retracing our steps, we were once again in pursuit of restaurants in the fine dining category. If you are a seafood lover, San Sebastian is the place to go. Situated on the Bay of Biscay and two riverbanks makes it a perfect place for delicious seafood. In one of the restaurant windows, we spied what we thought were very large shrimp. Most of the seafood had name plates but not the shrimp (?). In my best Tex-Mex Spanish, I asked a fellow window-shopper the name of the shellfish. In my Spanish, the word would be *camerones.* In San Sebastian language, the word is ***gambos.*** And that on we dined.

One lovely New Year's Eve was spent in San Sebastian. We found a delightful restaurant where we thought we would like to enjoy this festive evening. Approaching a waiter, who was speeding around as if on roller skates, we asked if we could make dinner reservations. With a sad face and negative head shake, the waiter explained that the only time we could be seated would be so very early—8:30 p.m. to be exact. As the folks in Spain begin their dining experience at about ten, we were told the eight thirty hour was probably unacceptable to us. Hallelujah, eight thirty was perfect, as we would have never made it to ten. In fact, these days we are close to dining during *the early bird special hour*. UGH!

Filled to the brim with gambos, crusty French bread with olive oil dipping sauce, and flan for dessert, we *waddled* back to the contentment of the luxurious Maria Cristina Hotel. Sometime near the middle of the night, we were awakened by a glorious male voice serenading in the street on his way home from his New Year's celebration. Usually, we hate to be woken up by outside noises, but this songfest was so beautiful that we felt it to be a perfect ending to a special New Year's Eve.

New Year's morning, clear and very cold, we wandered to the fishing docks prior to our leaving for another destination. It was there I took a photograph, which is one of my favorites to this day and hangs in our home. A year or so later, I was leafing through *Wine Spectator* magazine, only to find someone else had taken almost the *exact* same photograph I had, and possibly on the same day, as the sky and clouds were practically identical. I presume the photographer had probably sold their copy to the magazine for a fine sum! I still keep the magazine and like to compare the photographs from time to time. At least I feel good about the fact that at one time in my life, I was as competent as a published photographer.

Italy

There were places on my Italy bucket list that I hoped would be achieved, and I am still hoping. I have never been to Rome or Venice, and maybe that is a good thing. You see, both of those cities have a pigeon population that equal all persons residing in New York City, and I am *(secretly)* afraid of birds. Dad has come to know this, so he clears the path of the *monster sparrows* when they hop a bit too close to me. By the way, when did sparrows grow to the size of the endangered California condors? Or at least they look that way to me.

Our trips to Italy were made during the winter months, with our destinations being the Mediterranean Sea and Riviera. Our driving routes varied in that one took us from Germany, over Brenner's Pass into Austria and down to Italy. The other was, on recommendation from foreign associate Ulrich (previously mentioned), through Tyrol, which is special in its own German/Italian way. The area of Tyrol is different in that it is both Italian and German. When dining in a restaurant, the menu is written in both Italian and German and serves traditional German and Italian cuisine.

The Brenner's Pass route was usually piled high with snow and ice, but it was far safer than the Tyrol route, which had a two-lane road with many hairpin turns winding up a steep mountain, only to meet tour buses careening downward with *head-on* possibilities, if not probabilities. I recall one near-collision experience that had Dad negotiating a severe hairpin turn only to find a tour bus coming at us at full *head-on* mode. I grabbed the panic bar and closed my eyes, only to open them and find the bus had vaporized. To this day, I don't know what happened to the bus. I only know that my *personal angel* must have taken over and delivered us safely.

Where Is the Ocean?

La Spezia/Genoa

Driving over Brenner's Pass in the snow and ice had Dad and me aching for the warmth and sun of the Italian Riviera. Dad's usual driving plan was to look at a map, find a destination on or near the sea/ocean, and go along until he found a village that might have accommodations for the night. On one occasion, the city of La Spezia seemed to be just the destination.

After driving most of the day, we were anxious to reach the water and locate a hotel for the night. Taking the La Spezia exit off the A12, we began our venture into the city. There were road signs aplenty directing us to the La Spezia Port, where we knew, obviously, there would be water. As you know, my map-reading skills are somewhat limited (that's a puffery statement), but my reading of signs is par excellence (even in the dark). So read I did, leaving the driving to Dad. No matter how well we followed the signs, we always ended on the top of a big hill, with no exit except for the road we had just traveled. Many times we went down said hill only to begin our sign reading once again. And many times we found ourselves on top of the same hill, and the only water we saw was in the far distance.

Dad is one to never give up, but this time in the late evening, he decided we should go toward Genoa, which is a city worthy of many hotels. Weaving our way back to A12, we were off to Genoa. Thankfully, A12 had many signs to Genoa, and we took off down the road in hot pursuit. Even though the signage was good, we saw no city lights as we neared Genoa. In the dark of night, we spied a sign stating the airport was nearby. Now we all know there are hotels near airports—that is, except in Genoa. In fact, we didn't catch sight of the airport either.

So drive on, we did. Finally, we spied a rather large hotel near a railroad yard. The old and somewhat *rickety* hotel appeared to be ready to close for the winter. And in its closing, I prayed the wooden floors would be repaired, as each footstep was a symphony of *creaks,* which brought on wails of laughter from tired old me (laughing, sometimes hysterically, is my defense for pure exhaustion).

The hotel clerk did allow us a stay for the night and suggested a small restaurant, one block away, for a bit of dinner. As Italians and most Europeans eat their evening meal late in the day, we were assured the restaurant would be open. And sure enough, it was.

We were in Italy, so certainly we should eat spaghetti paired with a glass of Chianti. First let me say that no one in the restaurant spoke English except for me and Dad. After a bit of crude sign language, plus the word "spaghetti," we placed our order. This was most confusing, as the waiter kept motioning what else did we want to eat. Spaghetti is all that was needed, just like spaghetti we eat back in the good ole United States. It turns out that spaghetti, in Italy, is always a traditional first course in restaurants and the main meal should follow. Somehow we all came to an agreement that spaghetti was all we wanted, and the order was placed.

This brings to mind an old friend, Joe, whose parents were of direct Italian descent. Their Thanksgiving and Christmas turkeys were always preceded by a helping of spaghetti as the first course. In fact, probably most of their meals were served with spaghetti.

While waiting for our spaghetti fare, we noticed an unusual interior decorating feature. Pictures, all painted alike, were hung from the highest point on every wall in the dining area. Tired as we were, this observation, along with a tad of Chianti, put us in a cheerful mood—that is, until we were presented the bill.

Scribbled in Italian, of course, was the number 50,000 (lira). First of all, the waiter had no idea how much to charge just for spaghetti instead of a complete meal, and secondly, Dad had no idea how much fifty thousand *big ones* were. It's a good thing that Dad is not faint of heart, as I could see the wheels turning in his head as to how we might replenish our travel funds. As it turned out, the fifty thousand lira amounted to about fifteen dollars, and we were once again saved.

Walking back, we were grateful to have found our creaky old hotel and looked forward to a good night's sleep. The next morning while brushing my teeth, Dad yelled, "Mom, come here, quick." Running to the bedroom, I found Dad looking out of the window to view **THE BEAUTIFUL MEDITERRANEAN SEA.** Somehow, someway, we had found our way to our desired destination, the beginning of the Italian Riviera. Again, may I talk about the blind hog finding the acorn, and surely we did just that.

Don't Take the Key

Alassio

When reading guidebooks, one will find only about two paragraphs devoted to Alassio. Sadly, Alassio is no longer a sleepy fishing village, though it still possesses some old-world charm, colorful buildings with singing canaries on the porches, and a great beachfront promenade. Dad and I discovered Alassio quite by accident, even though my good friend Connie tells me there are no coincidences in life, only miracles. If she is correct, we were blessed to find Alassio along with a small and charming hotel by the water. This hotel became our ultimate destination for several years.

The hotel, which was owned and operated by a two-generation family, was small and simple in décor. The elevator was even smaller than the elevator in the Regina Hotel in Paris (I didn't think that was possible). With three people stuffed in the elevator, there was almost too much familiarity. There was a hotel desk where you registered and received a room key that was supposed to stay at the desk when you left the hotel. Now, come on, the key was attached to what looked like a full-size door knob and weighed at least one pound. Put that in your pocket and you risk serious physical damage. However, Dad once forgot and walked out the front door holding the key and was immediately approached by the clerk/daughter, who arm-wrestled the key away from him.

The tiny hotel had a dining room where three meals were served daily. After a day or so of experimental hotel dining, we determined breakfast would be our meal of choice, and we would then stroll through the village in hopes of finding other restaurants available for lunch and dinner. One breakfast ritual we came to enjoy was the mother/owner, who would stroll regally through the dining room each morning and bid every guest *buongiorno* (good morning). It appeared the daughter was the hotel manager and kept things running well. I am not sure what part the son played other than to put on his French beret, hoist his rather portly body onto a too-small motor scooter, and ride about the village smiling and waving.

By the way, motor scooters are a major means of transportation in Italy. In fact, there are so many on the streets that the noise is much like a swarm of bees getting ready to attack, and it is even worse in the large cities, such as Milan. Another form of transportation that is equally annoying is the three-wheel motor scooter enclosed much like a golf cart. You encounter these death traps on major roads doing a maximum speed of about 25 mph. These three-wheelers seem to appear, head-on, at every hairpin turn.

We were fortunate in Alassio that the beautiful beachfront promenade was directly in front of our hotel. As I mentioned earlier, the Germans are walkers. They walk and hike everywhere. They wear sturdy shoes and comfortable clothes for their walking. But they have nothing on the Italians. The Italian women dress to the nines when they parade the promenade. In winter, hats, fur coats (the real kind), and handmade shoes dress the women while proper jackets, shirts, ties, hats, and freshly polished shoes are worn by the men. Tiny shops, with their merchandise displayed out of doors, line the promenade. The shopkeepers bring their wares outside each morning and return them inside around noontime. After about a three-hour lunch/nap break, the shops reopen and all goods are, again, placed out of doors for sale. A great deal of unnecessary work I might say.

Residents of Alassio seem to eat their evening meal in restaurants. The folks usually have the same table, and any leftover wine from the previous meal is saved and served again. This brings to mind one mature couple who claimed ownership to a window table overlooking the sea. One evening, upon arrival for dinner, they found *their* table occupied. Refusing to be seated elsewhere, they left in a HUFF—maybe never to return again. Thankfully, we were not the ones who *trespassed* on sacred territory.

We haven't traveled to Alassio in sometime, but we wonder if the mother still marches through the breakfast room each morning with a smile and wishes each guest *buongiorno.*

Watch Out for the Horses

Siena

One of Italy's most beautiful landscapes is the centrally located city of Siena. Siena is filled with narrow streets and steep alleys and is often described as Italy's best preserved medieval city. Actually, it looks much like it did in the fourteenth century, or so I have been told. While walking the streets, you can see the medieval *contrade,* seventeen neighborhoods into which the city has been historically divided. Some symbols of the *contrade* are *tartaruga* (turtle), *oca* (goose), and *istrice* (porcupine).

Arriving late one Sunday afternoon, Dad and I began our ritual of finding a bed/hotel for the night. After several inspections, we were fortunate to find the Palazzo Ravizza, with space available. A ten-minute walk to the center of town seemed to be the proper thing to do on a beautiful and warm afternoon. Hardly a few minutes into our walk, we were *greeted* by throngs of people all shouting loudly. "What kind of riot is this?" I asked Dad. In order to save our lives, we sprinted our way to the safety of our hotel—at Olympic speed, I might add. While seeking safety and shelter, Dad and I managed to escape one of the most treasured events in the history of Siena, ***Il Palio.***

Aside from the fact we were almost trampled by bands of maniacal Italians, we were fascinated by the story of the event. The Palio is a horse race contested between Siena's *contrada*, which are the seventeen neighborhoods that have divided the city since the Middle Ages. The Sienese strongly identify themselves by the *contrada* where they were born and raised. At no time is this competition more fierce than at the time of the Palio.

The race itself is of raw and questionable character. There is barely enough room for the horses to run three laps on the makeshift campo course. Falls and collisions are inevitable. Danger abounds for horses, jockeys, and spectators as well. Horses are chosen at random three days prior to the race, and jockeys (who ride bareback) are mercenaries hired from surrounding towns. Bribery, secret plots, and treason are commonplace. In fact, the word for "jockey," *fatino*, has come to mean "untrustworthy" in Siena. Incidents of drugging (horses) and kidnapping (jockeys) are frequent and usual. Only disabling a horse's reins remains prohibited.

Once the race begins, it is over in a matter of a few minutes. The frenzied crowd then carries the winning jockey through the streets of the *contrada* he represented. In past tradition, the winning jockey was "entitled" to the girl of his choice. Today, the winning *contrada* will celebrate well into the night with food and drink. The champion horse is present as the guest of honor. The fact that Dad and I did not witness the race is of some question. I would have loved to experience the race, but I suppose living to tell the story is of more importance. I do wish to see great-grandchildren someday. However, being an avid animal lover, I am happy the horse got to celebrate in style.

Sometime after Dad and I recovered from our near-death experience at the hands of the overzealous Italians, we agreed that finding a spot for dinner should be our next goal. As we surely did not want to walk back in the direction of the city, we wound up our rental car in search of such a restaurant. Shaken still from our attack of the horserace people, we forgot that Italians normally dined at some ungodly late hour. Sure enough, not an open restaurant was to be found.

Agreeing to motor back to the hotel in hopes of possible room service, we spied a Pizza Hut look-alike that appeared to be opening their doors for business. Of course the usual—no Italian, no English. Spaghetti is always safe in Italy, and Dad pointed on the menu to Bolognese sauce—somewhat of a gamble I might add. In the confines of the small restaurant with thin paper napkins and no tablecloths, we dined on the best Italian food we had ever tasted. A lovely end to a rather exciting day.

England

My first visit to England was for an airplane change—with a one night layover—en route to Africa. Three lady friends and I were off to spend four adventuresome weeks in the African bush. From Houston to Nairobi, the flying time is twenty-four hours. Therefore, our trip was broken at the halfway point in London. My first day in London showed me the thrill of big-time shopping at Harrods. My three friends were well experienced with this and were good mentors. That evening, we went to the theater to see the musical *Evita.* I rather enjoyed the production, but my three friends did not particularly like it. I don't know how they could give an opinion, as they slept through most of it. Admittedly, it had been a rather long day. Actually, I have seen those same three friends *snooze* through the opera, where we had season tickets.

Our flight to Nairobi the following day was at midnight. Having a bit of spare time available, I arranged for a driver to show me the sights in London, and my three friends decided to join me. As luck would have it, this was on a Monday, and all museums, towers, etc., were closed. The Monday closure is almost worldwide. I asked driver Monty to show me London in a day, and he did—from outside the buildings. Monty did a good job, and we even stopped for a pint in a thatched-roof pub. I enjoyed my brief visit to London and promised myself I would return someday. Little did I know it would be fifteen years later with Dad.

By the way, friend Ida Jo and I used to say we would someday take our granddaughters to have tea with the Queen. Obviously, we did not. However, as I have said several times, if not for an accident of birth, I would be royalty.

The Train Is Broken

London

Several years previous to Mom, Dad had visited Bath and was certain I would love the excavated Roman baths, art galleries, and museums. With this in mind, Dad and I flew to London for a night prior to our leaving for Bath the next day—on the train. Dad said the English countryside was beautiful and that I would enjoy the ride. We both agreed that we were too old to be trying to drive on the wrong side of the road. In addition, did you know that all the equipment inside the auto is on the wrong side of the car—i.e., steering wheel, accelerator (left foot), gear shift (left hand), etc.? That was news to me!

Following breakfast the next morning, we walked upstairs to finish packing prior to our leaving for the train station. I am a noise person. I like to have soft noise around me most of the time, so upon entering our hotel room, I turned on the TV (tellie). Guess what! The morning news was full of information regarding a train derailment just outside Paddington Station, our station of departure. Not only were the trains not running, but the roads to Bath were also closed and would probably remain so for several days. I did find it quite curious that it took four days for Queen Elizabeth to visit the train wreckage site where there had been many casualties. It seems she was waiting for a *proper* platform to be erected so that she could be seen by all.

This left us three days in London before our scheduled flight to Munich. So sightsee we did. Dad is not a great sightseer, but

I must say he was a really good sport about my wanting to visit the touristy spots in London. Our first stop in London was Buckingham Palace. No, we didn't go inside the palace, but I did spend considerable time gawking. Then all of a sudden, miracle of miracles, the changing of the guard began, and we were on the front row! The pageantry was breathtaking. Here's that "blind hog/ acorn" business again. Another stop along the way was the Tower of London. Again, Dad was very patient while we toured the crown jewels. This is truly a girl thing.

As Dad had toured London many times, I thought I would ask to go somewhere he had not been. You guessed it, Harrods would be the place. I parked Dad in the restaurant with a bowl of soup, and off I went to explore each and every floor. I bought tote bags with the Harrods logo on them, coffee mugs with a cat and frog design, Christmas decorations, and two Harrods annual Christmas bears—one for me and one for my granddaughter.

The following day, after meeting with Dad's law associates, we strolled the mall (they pronounce it mell) and meandered by the River Thames (they pronounce it Tims)—what's wrong with those people? This provided a great view of Big Ben and the Parliament buildings. All of a sudden, Dad asked if I would like to have lunch on the *Queen Mary*. Dad must have had *connections* I knew nothing about—what a rascal that Dad. A bit farther down the riverbank path, we came upon the *Queen Mary*, or should I say Dad's *Queen Mary*. There in all its *peeling paint* glory was a semirefurbished boat of the TUGBOAT family. After all the strolling and meandering, lunch and a cool drink sounded *brilliant,* which is a word the Brits say with monotonous regularity. So eat and drink we did, and it was *lovely,* another of those overused British words.

With Germany in our sights, we made our way to a different hotel near the airport where we would depart for Munich. We had walked many miles (?) that day and were especially tired. Our room, located at the end of a *LONG* hallway, had the problem of not allowing the room key to open the door. I stood outside the door while Dad went to the registration desk to ask for a new key. This occurred two times! I could see Dad's temper nearing the boiling point. "Yes, Dad, I'll go this time." Off I trudged, with tired feet to ask for another key. This too did not work.

Again, I dragged my body to the registration desk and demanded a clerk accompany me with a workable key. With great apology, the clerk went with me, opened the door, and asked if she could order a beverage for us as their gift for the trouble. Dad asked for his vodka and grapefruit juice (pretty simple I say) and I asked for a Canadian Club and water (CC and water), also simple. Shortly, a knock on the door announced the arrival of our (save us) beverages. Sure enough, Dad's vodka and grapefruit drink was perfect, and mine consisted of one bottle of **Canada Dry ginger ale.** Even though we speak somewhat the same language as the British, we seem to have a problem with communication.

Our second visit to London was strictly to meet with Dad's law associate, take a pause in Harrods, and then on to the elusive Bath (by train). The vacation to Bath included a side trip to Cardiff for Dad to see the house where his father was born.

Bath

The Queen Has Thick Ankles

As previously mentioned, Dad had visited Bath on several occasions and was certain I would love the excavated Roman baths, art galleries, and museums. And he was correct. Following a successful (this time) train ride from London, we arrived in the lovely city of Bath. Bath is a grand Georgian town and is one of England's highlights. Checking into our proper British hotel (with good food), we began our trek (no rental car this time) into the heart of the city.

First on my bucket list for this trip was, of course, to see the Roman baths. The hot springs have drawn people here since prehistoric times, so I have read. It was on this site that the Roman patricians would gather to soak themselves, drink the mineral waters, and socialize. When the Romans left the area, the baths were abandoned and were partially covered.

In 1702 and 1703, Queen Anne visited the baths, and her frequency of visits inspired *medicinal* bathing to become the fashion. Again, *proper people* began to flock in to bathe and socialize. In the eighteenth century, the site was reopened. During the nineteenth century, the Roman bath complex was rediscovered and excavated. There is an excellent museum that contains a wealth of artifacts recovered during the excavation. But don't be fooled, the water is a *murky* pea green and tastes very bitter. However, I've been told the mineral waters have many curing qualities, such as healing arthritis and helping with infertility, as experienced by some British royalty. I don't know if you have to drink the water or rub it on to receive the *cure.*

Adjacent to the baths (hot springs) and complex is the famed Pump Room built in1792-1796. Bath society who liked to check on new arrivals to the city would *parade* up and down the Pump Room for hours looking at everybody and speaking to no one. Today, you can dine on a small lunch or sip tea (which we did) and, for a fee, taste the mineral water (which we did not). Would you pay money to taste pond scum that was infamously bitter?

The Royal Victoria Park was formally opened in 1830 with a visit from the eleven-year-old princess Victoria (who later became queen). A beautiful bronze statue of Queen Victoria oversees the park but was never viewed by the Queen. It seems that on her visit as a princess, someone noted she had *thick ankles.* This so infuriated the princess she never returned to Bath—even as queen. I really don't blame her much. She never even got to see the statue in her image, but we did. In fact, I have a photo of the statue with a plump pigeon sitting on the head.

This trip to Bath was Dad's first experience of riding a bus to see the sights. Dad has never wanted to take any type of tour—bus, cruise, walking, etc. Nearing the end of a day of walking and with our leaving the next day, we decided to take a city sightseeing bus that would take us around the city and immediate countryside. It was great to sit and have someone describe the sights of interest to us. I believe that now Dad is much more receptive to a tour in the future. YEAH!

In addition to Dad's wanting to show the Roman baths to me, he truly wanted to go on to Cardiff to try to discover the house where his father was born. And so we did.

Naughty but Nice

Cardiff

For some years, Dad had wanted to go to Cardiff in Wales in order to see the house where his father was born. We didn't know much, if anything, about the area; but as usual, we were up for the adventure.

Arriving by train and settling into a hotel just a block or two from major retail therapy, we began to hoof it toward the main center of town. As it was nearing late afternoon, we scurried as best we could to Cardiff Castle, one of the main attractions in Cardiff. As we walked closer to the castle, we began to view a scene of which neither of us had ever before witnessed.

There, on the lawn surrounding the castle, was a *MASS* of humanity who appeared to be mostly in the twenty-year age bracket. There were couples (boys to girls, boys to boys, and girls to girls) who were consuming alcoholic beverages of various classes, smoking who knows what (?), and listening to music (loud and heavy metal). They also seemed to be engaged in scandalous stages of *lovemaking.* As this was somewhat early in the evening hour, I was aghast to imagine what occurred as the sunset progressed into nighttime. We were to learn, a day or two later, that this behavior was acceptable and had become a Cardiff weekend *ritual.* We were SHOCKED and a little frightened. Staggering, we made our way to the retail therapy shopping mall, where we sat on a bench, sipped a soda, and attempted to regroup our thoughts. In conclusion, Dad and I wondered if what we had witnessed was an audition for *adult-only* films. Perhaps.

The following day, we planned to explore the countryside where Dad's father had been born. We were fortunate to locate a taxi driver who spoke English and appeared to have some knowledge of our intended destination (that blind hog thing again). A thought just occurred to me while writing this piece of fluff. I have referred to angels flying over us during our adventurous travels, and also I have referred, often, to blind hogs finding acorns. Maybe we should rethink the adage "when pigs fly." Perhaps there are pig angels too. At least there seem to be for Dad and me.

Our first stop on our ancestral journey was to a village pub. We had been told that a *very distant* relative of Dad's owned the pub and was usually there to greet neighboring folks. Unfortunately, this was Sunday afternoon, and the relative, of advanced age, had gone home for her afternoon nap. Dad and I were not sure where the relative perched on the family tree, but we took an obligatory photo in front of the pub to share with our family back home.

Second and most important stop was to find the house where Dad's father was born. Dad was eager to see the small cottage with thatched roof and fragrant antique rose garden. Our Welsh driver, with use of his GPS and several phone calls for help, managed to find the exact house of birth. And it was nowhere close to what Dad had expected.

To explain, historically, Cardiff and the surrounding areas were coal-mining territories. Cardiff, being on the sea, was a natural port for imports and exports. The adjoining areas were where coal was mined, and it was there, nearby, the families lived. The neighborhoods consisted of rows of brown brick, flat-faced, townhouse—type apartments. I'm sure Dad was somewhat disappointed not to find a village similar to the English Cotswold, but it was a time of endearment to see the birth house, and he was pleased.

Following a frenzied trip to the British patent office and dinner at a lovely restaurant by the sea, Dad and I were, once again, on our way to London and then to the United States the next day. Our favorite and only travel agent, Carol, had suggested we stay in a hotel adjacent to Heathrow Airport, as the early morning traffic in London can be *brutal.* Having experienced bumper-to-bumper traffic in London, we agreed that the airport hotel was a *brilliant* idea. (Remember the two overused words in Great Britain, *brilliant* and *lovely*?)

Stepping off the train we commenced to search for signs directing us to the airport hotel. None to be seen. Spying an information station, we asked for hotel directions. And sure enough, the agent was kind enough to point the way. After a short walk, we began to see small signs with arrows pointing the way to the hotel. So walk we did while dragging our luggage behind. About every thirty yards, we found another sign with the arrow leading us down another path. After approximately forty-five minutes later and two miles of exhausting ambulation, we found the hotel. Wiping the sweat from our brows, we collapsed onto comfortable chairs and sipped *medicinal beverages* for survival. Needless to say, the next morning we took a taxi to the airport terminal for our flight back home.

All in all, it was a *brilliant* trip filled with *lovely* memories.

Epilogue

When I look back and visit my memory bank about the many adventures Dad and I have shared, I can hardly believe all occurred in less than twenty years. Everything you have read is true (except for the extreme muffin-top body but it made for good reading), and yes, we were LOST much of the time. We still do travel but not as frequently as in the past. We continue to enjoy our fishing trips to Alaska, the annual visit to Germany, and a yearly stop in Santa Fe, where Dad has located the PERFECT sopapilla for excessive calorie consumption.

Our haven in Maui is a marvelous retreat from the rigors of everyday life. We would probably stay longer if our condominium allowed pets (not even cats) and we do miss our pup, Ruffles, when we are away from home.

We plan to continue our adventures as long as good health permits. Oh, by the way, our last trip home from Munich was a flight of pure excellence. Due to an oversold flight, Dad and I were *upgraded* to first class on a 777 aircraft. Again, the blind hog/acorn, or is it the pig angel, who made certain we were once more successfully flying BY THE SEAT OF OUR PANTS.